MISCELLANIES

(Second Series)

Peg Woffington.

MISCELLANIES

(Second Series)

BY

AUSTIN DOBSON

" *Non ulla Musis pagina gratior,*
Quam quæ severis ludicra jungere
Novit, fatigatamque nugis
Utilibus recreare mentem."

JOHNSON TO CAVE.

Essay Index Reprint Series

BOOKS FOR LIBRARIES PRESS, INC.

FREEPORT, NEW YORK

First published 1901
Reprinted 1967

LIBRARY OF CONGRESS CATALOG NUMBER:
67-28749

PRINTED IN THE UNITED STATES OF AMERICA

To
the Illustrator of
" The Ballad of Beau Brocade,"
and
" The Story of Rosina " : —
to
HUGH THOMSON,
these pages are inscribed
by
his attached Friend
AUSTIN DOBSON.

———————

" *Let Envy crave, and Avarice save ;*
Let Folly ride her circuit ;
I hold that—on this side the grave—
To find one's vein and work it,
To keep one's wants both fit and few
To cringe to no condition,
To count a candid friend or two—
May bound a man's ambition."

MAY, 1901.

PREFACE.

THE "Essays and Introductions" in Part I
of this Volume need no explanation. They
are, mainly, from that Eighteenth Century stock
which has supplied the majority of their prede-
cessors. They appeal to the same sympathetic
audience and they are subject to the same limi-
tations. For the "Occasional Verses and
Inscriptions" of Part II., on the contrary, a
word of preface is required. Some of them
have been composed since the poems included
in the series of which this is Volume Eleven,
were first collected ; one or two, incredible as
it may seem, were overlooked by their writer
when that collection was made ; others again,
though then intentionally omitted, have since
been enquired for by friendly readers. Finally,
a wish has been expressed in several quarters
that a few specimens of the little votive pieces
dispersed in various presentation copies of the

author's works, should have the advantage of a wider publicity. Thus it comes about that the last pages of the book, in the historic words of Mr. Wegg, "drop into poetry." May they fall upon ears as attentive as those of Mr. Nicodemus Boffin! Like Time, he was an eminent dust contractor, but at least he was appreciative.

AUSTIN DOBSON.

Ealing, May, 1901.

CONTENTS.

PART I.

ESSAYS AND INTRODUCTIONS.

PART II.

OCCASIONAL VERSES AND INSCRIPTIONS.

ix

PAGE.

Contents.

PART I.

ESSAYS AND INTRODUCTIONS.

MRS. WOFFINGTON.

THE readers of Walton's eloquent life of Donne will remember in what strange wise the great Dean of St. Paul's caused his last likeness to be drawn. Wrapped in a winding sheet "tied with knots at his head and feet, and his hands so placed, as dead bodies are usually fitted to be shrouded and put into the grave, . . . with his eyes shut, and with so much of the sheet turned aside as might show his lean, pale and death-like face"—he was depicted by " a choice Painter ; " and was thus afterwards carved in stone on the monument which stands in the southeast aisle of St. Paul's. The history of Art has seldom to record such unshrinking departures from the orthodox half and three-quarter lengths, looking to left or right, which people our galleries. But in the national collection at St. Martin's Place is a portrait which, in some measure, deviates as frankly from the conventional ; and yet belongs to an epoch far less imaginative than that of Donne. It represents a figure in a bed, the curtain of which is turned back. The heap

3

only is visible, and wears a small lace cap drawn
closely round the face, which is that of a handsome middle-aged woman, apparently in failing
health.   The hair, which shows underneath the
cap, is dark ; so are the eyes.   There is a faint
smile at the corner of the lips ; and a curious
indefinable impression is conveyed to the spectator that the head alone is alive, or, in other
words, that the body to which it belongs has
lost the power of motion.   This impression is
correct.   The painting, which is by Roubillac's
friend Arthur Pond, depicts the once-famous
actress, Margaret, or " Peg " Woffington, the
incomparable Millamant and Modish, the
unrivalled Wildair, of the Georgian stage ; the
accomplished and majestic Monimia, Calista,
Roxana, Palmira of a crowd of stately and
sonorous old-world tragedies.   It was executed about 1758, soon after its subject had
been suddenly struck down by paralysis, and
had definitely retired from Covent Garden
Theatre.   From a biographical point of view,
Mrs. Woffington's fate has been curious.   She
has been made (as one of her critics has said) the
heroine of a romance which is more than half a
memoir : she has been made the heroine of a
memoir which is more than half a romance.
The function of the following pages is more

practical, since they pretend to do no more than recapitulate the leading incidents of Margaret Woffington's career as they have been ascertained by her most recent biographers. Among these, in particular, must be mentioned the late Augustin Daly, whose sumptuous privately printed volume[1] collects and embodies, with the patience of a specialist and the loyalty of an enthusiast, all the known circumstances of the actress's life.

II.

AT some time between 1718 and 1728—for it does not seem practicable to fix the date exactly —a certain Madame Violante was in the habit of providing entertainment to those of the Dublin play-goers for whom the two established theatres in Aungier Street and Smock Alley had ceased to afford any adequate attraction. A Frenchwoman with an Italian name, Madame Violante was by profession a tumbler and tight-rope dancer, and had built a booth at the back of a house fronting upon Fownes's Court, and close to College Green. Here, among other daring feats by herself and company, she was accustomed, as a crowning exploit, to traverse the high rope with two baskets, each

[1] *Woffington : A Tribute*, New York, 1888.

containing a child, suspended to her feet.   That
this sensational exhibition—perhaps far less
dangerous than it seemed—was attended by
accident, is not recorded.   But history, discreet
as to the identity of one of the small occupants
of the baskets, has disclosed that of the other.
Her name was Margaret Woffington ; and she
was the elder daughter of a journeyman bricklayer, then dead, and of a living mother, who
took in washing.   When, by familiarity,
Madame Violante's periculous performance had
lost its interest, she left Dublin for other
towns ; and the dark-eyed child who had been
wont to swing beneath her, returned home once
more to cry "halfpenny salads" about the
streets, or to fetch water from the Liffey for
her mother, now keeping a small huckster's
shop in the poorest part of Ormond Quay.
The young gentlemen from College Green
patronised the tiny water-cress merchant with
the bright eyes and apt answers ; and by the
time the whirligig of Madame Violante's wander-
ings had brought her round once more to the
Irish capital, little Woffington was growing
into a graceful girl.   This, from what follows,
must have been in 1728 or 1729.   For it was
just at the period when London had gone
" horn mad " over the exceptional success of

John Gay's audacious *Beggar's Opera.* One of
the collateral developments of that success was
the representation of the piece by children ; and
Madame Violante, quick to shoot the flying
folly, promptly organised a Lilliputian *troupe*
for the Irish market. Little Peg Woffington
was cast for Polly ; and soon distanced all her
juvenile—one might almost say infantile—rivals,
not only by her native precocity, but by the
positive charm of her acting. Her supremacy
in this way was the more remarkable, because
the energetic Frenchwoman seems to have been
unusually fortunate in securing clever children
for her performers. Several of her pupils
subsequently became distinguished either on the
Irish or the English boards. Her Peachum
was a boy who grew into the more than
respectable comedian, Isaac Sparks ; John
Barrington was her Filch ; and Betty Barnes
(afterwards Mrs. Martin), her miniature
Macheath. To these Mr. Daly adds, as
Lockit, the solemn and highly-dignified Bensley ;
but here there must be some misconception,
for Bensley was not born. The success which
these small players obtained had curious results.
The Smock Alley company of grown-ups, jealous
of their youthful competitors, procured from the
Mayor an order to close Madame Violante's

establishment, upon the pretence that it was injurious to their own less popular efforts. Thereupon the Dublin people, with the opportune aid of the Earl of Meath, incontinently subscribed for the erection of a special theatre in Rainsford Street, beyond the pale of His Worship's jurisdiction; and here in 1729, the Lilliputians entered upon a fresh career of prosperity.[1]

For the Polly of the Violante *troupe* these things were not without their profit. She was far too young to marry a Duke as did her London rival, Lavinia Fenton; but by and by the managers of the Aungier Street house, certain clever brothers of the name of Elrington, began to take notice of the good-looking girl, to give her the run of the theatre, and to aid her generally in qualifying for what, to all appearance, was to be her special vocation in life. Madame Violante, too, continued to instruct her young friend, who was soon playing hoyden and other parts. From Madame Violante it must also have been that Peg Woffington acquired her

[1] History (especially stage history) repeats itself; and this conflict between Smock Alley and Rainsford Street recalls that earlier struggle, referred to in *Hamlet*, between Shakespeare's Company at the Globe and the Children of the Chapel—the " little eyases, that cry out on the top of question "—at the Blackfriars Theatre.

excellent knowledge of French; and no doubt the discipline of the French acrobat helped to improve and develop a figure that even in its unkempt infancy had been remarkable for its grace and symmetry. We next hear of her in connection with a play, a scene of which, perpetuated by Frank Hayman's brush, long decorated one of the old supper-boxes at Vauxhall. This was *The Devil to Pay ; or, the Wives Metamorphosed* of Charles Coffey, a deformed Dublin schoolmaster, who had already produced a ballad-opera in imitation of Gay. He had followed this up in 1731 by the above-mentioned piece, in which another excellent actress and later rival of Miss Woffington, Catherine Clive (then Miss Raftor) had made her first real hit at Drury Lane. The Dublin exponent of Nell, the Cobbler's wife, was Peg Woffington ; and her rendering of the part was entirely satisfactory both to the public and the author, who is said to have declared that she had done as much to make the character as he had. What was more, he persuaded the elder Elrington to take her into the Aungier Street company. The manager was nothing loth, and on the 12th February, 1734, Peg Woffington made her first appearance at the Dublin Theatre Royal in the part of Ophelia.

At this time, if the date of her birth be correctly given as 18th October, 1718, she was fifteen, and probably wore a costume in which she looked as absurd, to our eyes, as Iphigenia in the hoop of Madame de Genlis. She is affirmed to have been well-grown and tall ; and from her earliest picture, should already have been notably handsome.   Bricklayer's daughter though she was, she had an inborn distinction of her own which the Dublin ladies thought original enough to copy.   Her arms—said Mrs. Delany in later life—were " a little ungainly " ; but she seems to have really possessed the long tapering fingers, which, when hands were carefully painted in from models, recur so persistently in eighteenth-century portraits.   She had splendid dark eyes, under well-marked brows, and an arch expression heightened by her powderless hair, and the lace cap or flat garden hat, with which, from her numerous portraits, she knew how to set off the *grata protervitas* of her beauty.   That her voice was rather hard and unpleasing, seems to be admitted ; but, as she succeeded in ballad-opera, she must have contrived, in some way, to disguise its defects. In her busy progress from the Violante booth to the Aungier Street boards, she could scarcely, one would think, have found much time for cul-

tivation ; but she had somehow acquired a taste
in dress, which, combined with an uninherited
fine-lady air and an instinctive dexterity in the
use of a fan, sufficed to make her a fashion with
the women. The men, too, discovered that the
young actress from the little shop at Ormond
Quay was more than their match at repartee ;
and further, that although she was habitually
good-humoured, she was also thoroughly
capable of making herself respected. Lastly,
she was genuinely devoted to her profession,
scrupulously loyal to her business engagements,
and an irreproachable daughter to the homely
mother to whom she dutifully transferred her
theatrical earnings.

The change to the Aungier Street house,
however, did not materially increase these,
which Madame Violante had already raised to
the then magnificent stipend of thirty shillings
a week, the exact sum Rich had thought enough
for Lavinia Fenton. But the young comedian
gained largely in experience ; and the perfect
unconsciousness of her own good looks, to
which Murphy bears testimony, made improvement easier, for it did not prevent her from undertaking parts such as Mrs. Peachum and
Mother Midnight—assumptions which must
have involved considerable personal disfigure-

ment. From the Theatre Royal, after some temporary disagreement with Elrington, she went back to Rainsford Street, then occupied by a new company. But about 1738, she was again in the Theatre Royal. The little part of Sylvia in the *Recruiting Officer* had revealed to her the seductions of a masculine disguise; and in April of the year above mentioned, she performed for the first time the *rôle* with which, in the minds of many, she is mainly associated— that of Sir Harry Wildair in the *Constant Couple* of Farquhar. The *Constant Couple*, although witnessed by the blushing heroines of Miss Burney, is not a performance calculated to commend itself, in these days, to any but those who have accepted and absorbed Lamb's ingenious plea for the artificial comedy of the last century; and even during Mrs. Woffington's lifetime, there were not wanting those among her fervent admirers who regretted that so attractive an actress should have made choice of a " breeches part " for her most popular impersonation. Yet of her success as the Fantasio of the Augustan Age there can be no manner of doubt. Not only did she rival the first admirable creator of the character, Robert Wilkes, but she fairly drove Garrick himself from the field. Borrowing something from the

author, and adding something to that essentially
her own, she produced an "altogether" of
verve, piquancy, and vivacity, which, acquiring
its finishing touch from the fact that she was a
woman, rendered her absolutely irresistible to
her audience.   That, as Boaden affirms, she actually succeeded in making Farquhar's lively rake
"not only gay but innocent" is incredible ; but
she never had a serious competitor during her
lifetime, and managers invariably found "Mrs.
Woffington as Sir Harry Wildair" a charm to
conjure with.   It was as Sir Harry that Hogarth painted one of his many portraits of her.
This belonged to Mr. Daly, and renders full
justice to a pair of magnificent eyes which,
when animated, must have been as eloquent as
Garrick's.   At the Club which bears Garrick's
name, is another likeness of her by Hogarth, a
full length representing her upon a sofa in ordinary costume.   This is the likeness which
Lamb is said to have described as "dallying
and dangerous."   The Garrick Club has also
pictures of Mrs. Woffington by Eckhardt, Mer-
cier, and Benjamin Wilson, none of which, ex-
cepting the Eckhardt, seems to have been reproduced.

III.

AFTER her successful appearance as Sir Harry Wildair, history, without much trustworthy detail, but with a liberal allowance of decorative legend, transports Mrs. Woffington to England. Whatever were her reasons for leaving Dublin, —and, in all probability, they may be simply epitomised in the statement that she sought to better herself,—it is clear that in 1740 she was seeking employment in London. With considerable difficulty she obtained access to the all-powerful John Rich, then manager of Covent Garden, who, from his later account to Reynolds, would appear to have been completely conquered by the "amalgamated Calypso, Circe, and Armida" who invaded his sanctuary. "She was as majestic as Juno," he declared, "as lovely as Venus, and as fresh and charming as Hebe." Eventually, Rich gave his visitor an engagement, and on the 6th November, 1740, Miss (speedily altered in the bills to Mrs.) Woffington made her appearance at Covent Garden as Farquhar's Sylvia, with Theophilus Cibber as Captain Brazen. After Sylvia, she played Lady Sadlife in the *Double Gallant*, and Aura (another part involving male costume) in Charles Johnson's *Country Lasses*.

Lastly, " by particular desire," she took the town by storm as Sir Harry Wildair, which had never before been acted in London by a woman ; and it was at once admitted that, since the death of Wilkes, it had never been acted so well. " No more," wrote an enthusiastic votary of Thespis and Prior :—

> " No more the Theatre I seek
>   But when I'm promised there to find you ;
> All HORTON's merits now grow weak,
>   And CLIVE remains far, far behind you.

> " 'Tis thus the polished Pebble plays
>   And gains awhile some vulgar praises,
> But soon withdraws its feeble rays
>   When the superior Diamond blazes."

The second stanza shows the writer to be an imitator rather than a rival of the author of the inimitable verses "To a Child of Quality." But there can be no doubt that the young actress from Aungier Street not only eclipsed the beautiful Christiana Horton, but obscured the new-risen star of Catherine Clive. Before the close of the season, Mrs. Woffington had appeared in six or seven parts, including those of Phyllis in Steele's *Conscious Lovers* (with its delightful window-cleaning scene), and of the all-popular Cherry in the *Beaux' Stratagem.*

Finally, for the benefit of Chetwood the prompter, then languishing in the King's Bench prison, she played Lœtitia in the *Old Batchelor* to the Fondlewife of her lifelong admirer, the veteran Colley Cibber, whose famous *Apology* was unhappily some months old, or he might have included in its pages a pen-sketch of his new colleague, fully equal to the admirable vignette which he draws of Mrs. Verbruggen as that " finish'd Impertinent." Melantha, in Dryden's *Marriage à-la-Mode*.　By this date, Mrs. Woffington's position was secured ; but, although she was too conscientious an artist to be a failure in anything, it was the novelty of the *rôles* of Sylvia (in the red coat and hat *bien troussé* of Captain Pinch), and of Sir Harry Wildair that most attracted her audience.　In this, her first season, she performed the latter part no fewer than twenty times—a considerable test of its popularity—and always to crowded houses.　It is true that Walpole styles her "a bad actress," and his friend Conway " an impudent Irish-faced girl."　But this was probably for the pleasure of being in a superfine minority, since both testify to her extraordinary popularity.　Walpole says she is " much in vogue " ; Conway that " all the town is in love with her."

On the 19th of May the season came to an end, and with it ended Mrs. Woffington's engagement to Rich. Why that usually astute personage permitted her to leave him is unexplained, but in the ensuing September she was acting Sylvia at Drury Lane. This she followed up by Lady Brute in the *Provoked Wife*, and she also appeared in more than one of Shakespeare's comedies, notably as Rosalind in *As You Like It*, when the Celia was Mrs. Clive, and the Touchstone, Macklin. She showed her kindness of heart by tenderly nursing one of her sick colleagues, William Millward, and when he died, she played for his widow and children. But the event of this time was the growth of her acquaintance with Garrick, who, after his successful entry into the profession in October, 1741, had been invited by Fleetwood to Drury Lane. There can be no question that from the first he was impressed by the charm and vivacity of the beautiful young Irishwoman, and it is also certain that she fully appreciated the supreme genius of the equally youthful actor (he was then but twenty-six, and only two years older than herself) who, at a bound, had risen to the kingship of the English stage. On Garrick's side, admiration prompted some of those metrical tributes which he pro-

duced with such facility on all occasions, and
his verses to "Sylvia" and "Lovely Peggy,"
are still to be read in the *London*, and other
contemporary magazines.

> "Were she arrayed in rustic weed,
>   With her the bleating flocks I'd feed,
>   And pipe upon mine oaten reed
>   To please my lovely Peggy.
>   With her a cottage would delight,
>   All's happy when she's in my sight,
>   But when she's gone 'tis endless night—
>   All's dark without my Peggy."

He acted Lear to his Peggy's Cordelia at
Drury Lane on the 28th May, 1742; and in the
following June they were both at Dublin, playing in the new theatre which had taken the
place of the Smock Alley building, and to
which they had been hastily summoned by the
manager, Duval, in order to counteract the
rival attractions of Quin and Mrs. Cibber at the
Theatre Royal. As might be expected, they
carried all before them. Mrs. Woffington as
Silvia, Mr. Garrick as Captain Plume ; Mrs.
Woffington as Lady Anne, Mr. Garrick as
"crook'd back'd Richard,"— were attractions
to which Mrs. Cibber as Indiana and Quin as
Young Bevil (in the *Conscious Lovers*) could
make no effectual reply. So crowded indeed

were the houses, and so sultry the season, as actually to bring about a kind of epidemic which Dublin playgoers christened the " Garrick fever."

At Dublin Mrs. Woffington definitely added to her repertory what was later to be one of her most successful parts, that of Lady Betty Modish in the *Careless Husband*. While Garrick hurried back to London with Mrs. Cibber, she remained in Ireland to arrange for the education abroad of her younger sister, Mary, and also to select a suitable retreat for her mother, whom O'Keeffe remembered years afterwards as a respectable old lady in a velvet cloak, with a diamond ring and an agate snuff-box, going the round of the Roman Catholic chapels, and chatting with her neighbours, no doubt upon the favourite topic of her famous daughter. Not long after Mrs. Woffington returned to London, she set up that curious joint establishment with Macklin and Garrick, and then with Garrick alone, which has exercised so many pens. The triple alliance was at Macklin's, No. 6 Bow Street, Covent Garden (which, by the way, had been built by the original Wildair, Wilkes) ; the dual association, in Southampton Street, Strand. Garrick was to play the part of paymaster ; the lady was to act as hostess.   But Garrick's conception of his *rôle* is alleged to have been mean, not to say miserly; Mrs. Woffington, on the contrary, was over profuse.   " She made the tea too strong," said Johnson to Mr. Scott, recalling those days; and Roscius grumbled at her wastefulness. Relating the story to Reynolds, the Doctor added a further detail to Garrick's grievance. " It [the tea] was as red as blood," he protested.   Nevertheless, the combined arrangement lasted for a considerable period; and, at one time (says report), even bade fair to ripen into a more permanent bond.   But which, in this connection, was " *l'un qui baise*," and which " *l'autre qui tend la joue*," is, at this date, difficult to affirm; and an impartial critic may perhaps be pardoned for wondering whether, on the gentleman's side, at all events, disinterested affection formed as important an element as identity of aim and ambition.   If—as Murphy and others maintain—the wedding-day was actually fixed, nothing would be more likely than that, as the inevitable hour approached, his native prudence should become more urgent in reminding Garrick that a lady whose hospitality was lavish, and whose admirers were legion, was not precisely the person to promise or promote a cloudless domesticity.   His passion

must have cooled appreciably as he thought of
these things, and his doubts grew darker in
proportion. At last he spoke out. He was
wearing the shirt of Deianira—he ruefully confessed. Whereupon Mrs. Woffington (who had
a fine spirit of her own), at once begged him to
put off that classical but uncomfortable garment,
and never to see her more, " except in the course
of professional business, or in the presence of a
third person." The gifts which had been ex-
changed between them were sent back; but
Gossip, already maliciously preoccupied with
the great actor's petty weaknesses, asserts that
he could not bring himself to part with a pair
of diamond shoe-buckles which had been one
of the lady's *gages d' amour*. A year or two
later he married Mlle. Eva Maria Violette.
Lady Burlington's *protégée* had no claim to be
compared in charm or talent with her husband's
first—or, more probably, his earlier—love ; but
she worshipped her " Davy," alive and dead,
with a persistent devotion which Garrick could
scarcely have hoped from the brilliant but vary-
ing and very mutable Mrs. Woffington.

During her connection with Garrick, Peg
Woffington continued to act at Drury Lane.
The records speak of her successes as Lady
Townly in the *Provoked Husband;* as Portia ;

as Mrs. Ford (there is a charming picture of
her by Haytley in this character) ; as Millamant in the *Way of the World ;* as Mrs. Frail
in *Love for Love.*   Nor did she confine herself
to impersonations which were morally or physic-
ally attractive.   She played Lady Pliant in the
Double Dealer ;   she played Mrs. Day in
Howard's *Committee,* not scrupling in this latter
part, says Tom Davies of Russell Street, "to
disguise her beautiful countenance, by drawing
on it the lines of deformity, and the wrinkles of
old age ; and to put on the tawdry habiliments
and vulgar manners of an old hypocritical city
vixen."   One of her rivals at the theatre even
at this time was Mrs. Clive, and little love
appears to have been lost between these queens
of the green-room.   "No two women of high
rank ever hated one another more unreservedly,"
says the honest chronicler above quoted.
". . . Woffington was well-bred, seemingly
very calm, and at all times mistress of herself.
Clive was frank, open and impetuous ; what
came uppermost in her mind, she spoke without
reserve : the other blunted the sharp speeches
of Clive by her apparently civil, but keen and
sarcastic replies ; thus she often threw Clive off
her guard by an arch severity which the warmth
of the other could not parry."   That she was

"at all times mistress of herself," is, however, to say too much, since once when *Henry the Fourth* was being played, these animosities culminated in an actual combat, in which admirers on either side freely engaged, to the huge joy of the caricaturists, who commemorated the fray in a plate called "The Green Room Scuffle." After the rupture with Garrick, strained relations with that now powerful personage were added to Mrs. Woffington's other tribulations, although fortunately he was not always acting at Drury Lane. But when, in 1747, he became co-patentee of that theatre with Lacy, and reinforced the ranks of its leading ladies by importing Mrs. Cibber and Mrs. Pritchard from Covent Garden, the situation became too difficult to maintain with dignity. Consequently, on the 15th April, 1748, Mrs. Woffington took her leave of Drury Lane as Phyllis in Steele's *Conscious Lovers*, and started for Paris to investigate the methods of the Théâtre Français, and more particularly the tragic method of that most accomplished tragic actress, Mlle. Marie-Françoise Dumesnil, then or but recently promoted from soubrette parts to the more important *rôle* of *mère*. To Mlle. Dumesnil, Garrick later gave the praise, so often applied to himself, of being, and not acting, the character assumed. But Gibbon, who had seen her frequently, was less enthusiastic. He preferred the " consummate art " of her rival, Mlle. Clairon.

When, after a prolonged vacation, Mrs. Woffington returned from the French capital, she betook herself to Covent Garden and to her old manager Rich, playing, in addition to her comedy parts, a good many fresh tragic characters, in which she shewed the not entirely salutary influence of her studies in the French School. One of these was Anne Oldfield's famous *rôle* of Andromache in the *Distressed Mother*. Another was Veturia in the *Coriolanus* of Thomson. But although she had escaped the Clive, Pritchard and Cibber coalition at the other house, she found at Covent Garden a fresh antagonist in the person of Dodsley's Cleone, the beautiful and blue-eyed George Ann Bellamy, a rival as aggravating as, and far more mischievous than, any member of the elder trio. The record of the sumptuary feud that presently arose between Mrs. Bellamy and Mrs. Woffington recalls, in some of its details, Steele's pleasant story of Brunetta and Phyllis, with the difference that the injured Brunetta (Mrs. Woffington) seems to have gone to the length of personally chastising her malicious competitor. Fortunately, Mrs. Bellamy was speedily abducted by one of her numerous admirers, and for a time Mrs. Woffington reigned at Covent Garden without dispute. Then, unhappily, Mrs. Cibber returned from Drury Lane, and discord began once more under a manager who, unlike Garrick, was entirely without the art of controlling those extremely " kittle cattle," tragedy queens.

> " He umpire sat,
> And by decision more embroil'd the fray,"—

quotes Tom Davies from the neglected pages of *Paradise Lost.* But we may turn from these dissensions to one of the few authentic anecdotes which help to eke out a picture of Mrs. Woffington. Once, when Rich had angered her by his tactlessness, she refused point-blank to act as a substitute for the always-ailing Mrs. Cibber ; and, as ill-luck would have it, the displeasure of the audience fell entirely upon her own devoted head. When she appeared as Lady Jane Grey they showed it. " Whoever," says Tate Wilkinson, " is living, and saw her that night will own that they never beheld any figure half so beautiful since. Her anger gave a glow to her complexion, and even added lustre to her charming eyes. They treated her very rudely, bade her ask pardon, and threw orange peels. She behaved with great resolution, and treated their rudeness with glorious contempt. She left the stage, was called for, and with infinite persuasion was prevailed on to return. However, she did, walked forward, and told them she was there ready and willing to perform her character if they chose to permit her ; that the decision was *theirs—on* or *off*, just as they pleased, a matter of indifference to her." The " ons " had it, continues the narrator, " and all went smoothly afterwards." But the last words are exact only as far as that particular evening was concerned, for in short space Mrs. Woffington quitted Covent Garden, and went back to her native island.

Henceforth her career may be more rapidly summarised. When she arrived at Dublin she was without an engagement. But at this time the Smock Alley Theatre was in the hands of Sheridan's father, whose leading lady was the Mrs. Bland to whom Lamb refers in " Old China." Sheridan was easily persuaded to enlist the services of Mrs. Woffington, and to inaugurate a success for himself. This was apparently the most popular period of Mrs. Woffington's life, for her performance of no more than four parts, Lady Townly, Maria,

Hermione, and Sir Harry Wildair, brought the Smock Alley House four thousand pounds, a larger sum than any theatre had previously gained with stock pieces. Other parts which she played were Cleopatra, Lady Betty Modish, Rosalind, Hypolita, Jane Shore, and Phyllis, certainly a very varied list. She was excellent in all; but in the comedy and fine-lady parts she was supreme. Never was such a Modish, such a Townly! With her Irish compatriots her popularity was unbounded, and, in an evil hour it was crowned by her election to the Presidentship of Sheridan's Beef Steak Club, an association which he had modelled on the London Association with a similar title, then some fifteen years old. Nothing could persuade the public, however, but that Sheridan's project had a concealed political significance. This belief they transferred to the Smock Alley performances and investing certain lines in Voltaire's *Mahomet* with a veiled reference to the Court party, proceeded to raise a riot and wreck the house. Mrs. Woffington's persuasive powers were invoked, but without effect. Sheridan's enterprise came to an untimely end, and Mrs. Woffington returned to London, where she still had admirers more steadfast and more phlegmatic than her excitable fellow-countrymen.

On the 22d October, 1754, she was again playing at Covent Garden in one of her old parts,
that of Maria in *The Nonjuror.*

IV.

As must have been gathered from the opening
pages of this paper, Margaret Woffington had
begun her theatrical career betimes.   When she
made her *début* in Madame Violante's basket
(an incident upon which the conscientious
biographer will not insist too strongly), she
can have been little more than a baby.   When
she played Polly Peachum she was ten or eleven ;
she was fifteen when she appeared as Ophelia
at the Aungier Street Theatre.   Untiring in her
devotion to her profession, she had also lived
the full life of an energetic and emotional nature,
and by the time she had reached her thirty-
eighth year, it was manifest that, although her
enthusiasm remained unabated, her exuberant
vitality was becoming exhausted.   She acted
Celia in the *Humorous Lieutenant ;* she acted the
Queen in *Richard III ;* she essayed, not successfully, Garrick's famous part of Lothario in the
Fair Penitent; she acted Lady Randolph in a
brand-new tragedy which an obscure Dr. Goldsmith reviewed in the *Monthly Review*—the deep-
mouthed *Douglas* of that Rev. John Home, in

whom dwellers north of the Tweed sought to discover a Scottish Shakespeare. Readers of *The Virginians* will recall a pleasant chapter in Thackeray's book where the Lambert family with George and Harry Warrington go to Covent Garden to see the Presbyterian gentleman's masterpiece. But although Miss Theodosia's soft heart is touched by Mrs. Woffington's " beauty and acting," the author of the novel is true to tradition in abstaining from putting her praises into the mouth of any critical member of the little party. She created the character of Lady Randolph, it is true, but it was not one of her successes.

It had been upon her own benefit, March 24, 1757, that she had played Lothario. A few weeks later, she had made her last appearance. Tate Wilkinson, an eye-witness upon this occasion, has described in his *Memoirs* what took place, in words which it is needless to paraphrase. On May 3d *As You Like It* was being given for the benefit of some of the inferior actors. " I was standing near the wing "—says Wilkinson—" as Mrs. Woffington in Rosalind, and Mrs. Vincent in Celia, were going on the stage in the first act. . . . She [Mrs. Woffington] went through Rosalind for four acts without my perceiving she was in the least disordered, but in the fifth act she complained of great indisposition. I offered her my arm, the which she graciously accepted. I thought she looked softened in her behaviour, and had less of the *hauteur* [Wilkinson had been unlucky enough to incur her displeasure]. When she came off at the quick change of dress, she again complained of being ill ; but got accoutred, and returned to finish the part, and pronounced in the Epilogue Speech, " If it be true that good wine needs no bush—it is as true that a good play needs no epilogue," etc., etc. But when arrived at " If I were among you I would kiss as many of you as had beards that pleased me," her voice broke, she faltered, endeavoured to go on, but could not proceed—then in a voice of tremor screamed, O God! O God! [and] tottered to the stage door speechless, where she was caught. The audience of course applauded till she was out of sight, and then sank into awful looks of astonishment, both young and old, before and behind the curtain, to see one of the most handsome women of the age, a favourite principal actress, and who had for several seasons given high entertainment, struck so suddenly by the hand of death, in such a situation of time and place. . . ."

She lingered for nearly three years from that

fatal night ; but never again appeared behind the
footlights. The theatrical calling was exposed to
great temptations, she told a young Teddington
friend who consulted her as to that profession ;
and it would be idle to contend that her own life
—a life of many *liaisons*—had been either worship-
ful or blameless. But her days henceforth were
passed quietly and decorously in her house by
the Thames (Teddington Place, now Udney
Hall), where she had for companion a Mrs.
Barrington, widow of the John Barrington who,
as a boy, had acted with her in the *Beggar's
Opera* at Dublin. During this period she is
said to have come under the influence of
Wesley ; but, as Mr. Daly has pointed out,
she had a clerical relative in the Hon. Mr.
Cholmondeley, her sister Mary's husband, who
had quitted the army to enter the Church, and
who is just as likely to have turned her thoughts
in serious directions, if her own calamity had
not been sufficient to do so. In any case, even
when she partially recovered, she neither sought
to renew her old triumphs nor to revisit the
scene of them. On the contrary, she is said
to have occupied herself in charitable offices,
and in knitting stockings which she distributed
periodically to the Teddington poor. She died
at last, on the 28th March, 1760, at a house in

Queen Square, Westminster (no doubt that of
her sister), where she was staying, and she was
buried in the graveyard of the little patchwork
parish church of St. Mary at Teddington, whose
then incumbent was the " plain Parson Hales "
of Pope, a rigourist who still compelled his
erring parishioners to do public penance for
their misdeeds. The actual site of her tomb
is now unknown ; but a tablet now on the
north wall of the chancel, at the back of the
reading-desk, records the interment " near
this Monument " of " Margaret Woffington,
Spinster." Probably this memorial was erected
by Mrs. Cholmondeley, since it includes an inscription to one of her own children, who had
died some time before. Mrs. Woffington's
property, when due provision had been made
for an annuity of £40 to her mother, went to
Mrs. Cholmondeley, and amounted to four
thousand pounds. John O'Keeffe, the drama-
tist, who was living at Teddington in 1794, affirms that she there built and endowed a number
of almshouses. But Lysons, writing a few
years later, says nothing of these ; nor is there
any mention of them in the Parliamentary
Report of 1824 on the Charities of Middlesex.
Meanwhile—for the better comfort of picturesque tradition—at the east end of the High

Street, next the post-office and near the Church, there exists to this day a low range of old-fashioned, wistaria-clad dwellings, with dormer windows, and tiny front-gardens, which continue to be known to the neighbourhood and the local directory as " Margaret Woffington's Cottages."

THE "GRUB STREET" OF THE ARTS.

THAT " fine madness " of incongruity which
tempted Charles Lamb into laughter at a
funeral, led him,—says his best biographer,—
at the top of Skiddaw, to think upon a certain
ham-and-beef shop in St. Martin's Lane.[1]
Where was this favoured and fortunate ham-
and-beef shop ? And where, under reconstruc-
tions and renewals, is the St. Martin's Lane of
Lamb ?—the St. Martin's Lane of the last century ? " It butteth," says honest John Strype in
his Stow of 1720, " on Northumberland House
in the Strand, and runneth Northwards beyond
Long Acre, and the new Buildings in Cock and
Pye Fields." In other words, it extended from
the southern end of the present Little St. Andrew Street (the site of the old Cock and Pye
Tavern), past Long Acre and St. Martin's
Church, to a spot in the Strand then opposite
Northumberland House, but now at the entrance of Northumberland Avenue. This was
the St. Martin's Lane of 1720 ; and judging
from Evans's map, it was also the St. Martin's

[1] *Charles Lamb*, by Alfred Ainger, 1888, p. 72.

Lane of 1799.[1] Sixty years ago, its limits had
become contracted. It had been cut into at
Long Acre by a continuation of Cranbourn
Street, and its southern boundary was the then
newly completed Trafalgar Square. Ten years
later still, directories give the southern termi-
nation as Chandos Street and Hemings' Row.
Hemings' Row—the "Dirty Lane" of our
grandfathers—disappeared in 1889 with the
creation of Charing Cross Road, but Chandos
Street still ends the eastern side of the Lane,
and serves to link the old thoroughfare with
Strype's description. For it was just above
Chandos Street that stood an ancient turnpike,
to which Steele seems to allude in his " Ramble
from Richmond to London." In that delightful " Voyage où il vous plaira " he relates how,
out of pure idleness, he diverted himself by following in " an Hack " the hack of a handsome
young lady with a mask and a maid. The
damsel's chariot was travelling " through Long
Acre towards St. James's." " Thereupon," says
the vivacious essayist, " we drove for King-street,
to save the Pass at St. Martin's Lane." At the
end of Newport Street and Long Acre the ve-
hicles become entangled, and for a moment he

[1] A facsimile of Evans's " New and Accurate Plan " was
issued with Kelly's " London Directory " for 1899.

gets a glimpse of his charmer " with her Mask
off." The chase continues " in all Parts of the
Town " for an hour and a half, when the quarry
is discovered to be a " Silk-Worm," which is
your hackney-coachman's term for those profit-
able fares " who ramble twice or thrice a Week
from Shop to Shop, to turn over all the Goods
. . . without buying anything." So Captain
Richard Steele, after a few more vagrom experiences, goes home to scribble his " Spectator "
thereon (it is No. 454, for Monday, August
11th, 1712), and, if possible, to explain his erratic
proceedings to his " Absolute Governesse " at
her new residence in Bloomsbury Square.

The site of the turnpike house here referred
to is supposed to have been 28, the first number
on the eastern side of the Lane. But the more
important buildings were on the western side,
and with the western side it is convenient to begin. Just beyond Parr's Bank and the present
Free Library was Peter's Court, which Strype
describes as " a very handsome and gentile
Place, with good Houses, well contrived, with
little Gardens to them,"—a state of things not
very easy to conceive at present, as Peter's Court,
which must have gone back as far as the Garrick
Theatre, and the narrow entrance to which was
between Nos. 111 and 110, has now given place

to the establishment of Messrs. Chatto and Windus. In Peter's Court, or at its entrance, was one of the many coffee-houses known as "Tom's," and even, if we may believe Mr. John Ashton,[1] the best known of them, although that distinction is generally claimed for "Tom's" in Russell Street, already referred to in the "Tour of Covent Garden."[2] But the most memorable building in Peter's Court must have been the dancing school which afterwards became the first studio of Monsieur Louis-François Roubillac, the sculptor, who, according to contemporary prints, there carved the statue of Handel in the character of Orpheus which so long ornamented the gardens at Vauxhall. The Handel is said to have been the first original work Roubillac executed in England, and the date of its erection, May, 1738, fixes that of his residence in Peter's Court. How much longer he remained there is unrecorded, but his old studio was subsequently, for a long period, the home of the St. Martin's Lane Academy of which we hear so much in the middle of the last century. At the death of Sir James Thornhill, the material of his drawing

[1] "Social Life in the Reign of Queen Anne," 1883, p. 174.

[2] "Eighteenth Century Vignettes," Third Series, p. 339.

school in James Street, Covent Garden, came
into the hands of his son-in-law, Hogarth.
"Thinking," says Hogarth, "that an academy
conducted on proper and moderate principle
had some use, [I] proposed that a number of
artists should enter into a subscription for the
hire of a place large enough to admit thirty or
forty people to draw after a naked figure."
The former dancing school in Peter's Court
exactly answered to these requirements, and
Hogarth lent his coadjutors Sir James's furniture. It was in this institution, of which
Michael Moser was the treasurer and manager,
and of the interior of which Hogarth himself
painted a picture, now at Burlington House,
that the majority of the artists of the reigns of
George II and George III received or completed their educations. Reynolds, Ramsay,
Zoffany, Wilson, Hayman, Cosway, Roubillac
himself, Nollekens, and a host of minor names,
were all scholars in this school, whose career of
usefulness only ceased with the establishment in
1769 of the Royal Academy, to which its "ana-
tomical figures, busts, statues, etc.," were in
course of time transferred.

After the St. Martin's Lane Academy had
vacated its old quarters in Peter's Court, the
great room was pulled down and rebuilt as a

Friends' Meeting House. Whether it was here that—*en route* for the ham-and-beef shop—Lamb made those studies of " uncommunicating muteness," which he has described so vividly in his " Essays," his editors say not. But a Friends' Meeting House continued to occupy the site of Roubillac's old studio until far into the present century, when, with the march of renovation, it moved to the eastern side of the Lane. Beyond the site of Peter's Court is the Duke of York's (formerly the Trafalgar Square) Theatre, which extends over the ground once occupied by Nos. 107 to 103, a space with many artistic memories. Here, for instance, at or " behind No. 104," lived Sir James Thornhill, in a large house with a grand allegoric staircase painted by himself. One of his successors was John Van Nost, son of the Van Nost of Piccadilly, who rivalled Cheere in leaden figures, and who was credited with that egregious gilt statue of George I which once adorned the enclosure at Leicester Fields. Another tenant of the same house was Frank Hayman, Hogarth's crony and co-decorator at Vauxhall, who filled so many eighteenth century books with noses *à la* Cyrano and spindle-shanks. (His own legs, by the way, were probably his model, if one may judge from those of Viscount Squanderfield in the " Marriage *A-la-Mode*,"

for whom he was the admitted sitter.)   A jovial,
careless boon-companion, he grew gouty as he
grew older, and though, like Thornhill, he
migrated ultimately to Dean Street, Soho, it
may well have been in St. Martin's Lane that
occurred the incident which Pyne relates in the
"Somerset House Gazette."   When Hayman
was engaged upon one of the large canvasses for
Tyers' New Room next the Rotunda at Vauxhall—it would seem to have been that in which
Britannia was represented distributing laurels to
certain distinguished officers—the Marquis of
Granby, who sat by Tyers' request to the artist,
and had heard of his past prowess as a pupil of
Broughton, proposed a preliminary set-to with
the gloves.   Hayman pleaded that he was old
and infirm.   But Lord Granby maintained that
he, too, was no longer a chicken, and, moreover,
that he was out of practice owing to his absence
in Germany.   The pair began accordingly, and,
after a magnificent display of science on either
side, Hayman, warming with the game, " got
home " so effectually on the " bread basket " of
the noble and gallant Marquis that they both,
being heavy men, came to the ground with a
terrific crash.   Thereupon Mrs. Hayman (she
had been the widow of Frank's friend, Fleetwood, the Drury Lane manager), rushing

frantically upon the scene, discovered her husband and the illustrious hero of Minden " rolling
over each other on the carpet like two enraged
bears."[1]

The year of Minden fight is 1759, and the
date of the hand-to-hand conflict in which the
popular warrior, whose bald head and blue
uniform decorated half the signs in the kingdom,[2]
figures so ingloriously must consequently be
placed later. But the house " behind No.
104," or No. 104 itself, had another resident
who is more eminent than either Hayman or
Thornhill. In 1753, according to Malone, Sir
Joshua Reynolds, then plain " Mr.," took up his
abode at a house in the Lane described as
" nearly opposite to May's Buildings " (on the
eastern side), and "nearly opposite to May's
Buildings " must have been a pretty accurate
indication of No. 104. Reynolds had not long
returned from Italy, painting, as his franker
friends informed him, in a manner that could
never succeed, since it was not in the least like
the manner of Kneller. Posterity has not confirmed that sagacious prediction. Unfortunately

[1] " Somerset House Gazette," 1824, i. 78.
[2] Readers of " Pickwick " will recall the " Marquis of
Granby " at Dorking, where Mr. Weller senior admin-
istered such condign punishment to the luckless Shepherd.

for our paper, however, Reynolds made only a brief stay in St. Martin's Lane, and there is no existent list of his sitters at this date. But the first portrait he painted after his establishment in London was that of his assistant, Guiseppe Marchi, the Italian boy who had accompanied him from Rome, and who, eventually, after a probation in the Peter's Court Academy, became himself an indifferent painter and a capable engraver. It was, in fact, Marchi's picture in a turban and oriental dress, now at Burlington House, which prompted the unfavourable criticism quoted above. No very notable incident concerning Reynolds' residence at No. 104 has been recorded, and in the same year (1753) in which he came to it he moved higher up on the left to No. 5, Great Newport Street, the only other London dwelling he occupied until his final migration to No. 47, Leicester Fields. But it was at St. Martin's Lane that he was joined by his youngest sister, Frances, whose artistic attempts made other people laugh and her brother cry, and who figures in Boswell's pages as the " Renny dear" of Johnson.

> " I therefore pray thee, Renny dear,
> That thou wilt give to me,
> With cream and sugar soften'd well,
> Another dish of tea,"—

sang the great man, in disrespectful parody of
Percy's " Reliques." He left her a book in his
will, and loved her fondly in spite of her fidgetty
peculiarities. At this date, however, Johnson
was not yet known to Reynolds, whose acquaintance he only made after Reynolds had removed
to Great Newport Street.

Four doors beyond No. 104, lived the por-
trait-painter John Cartwright, a mediocrity
whose chief claim to remembrance lies in the
circumstance that he had been, while at Rome,
the fellow-student of the fantastic genius Henry
Fuséli, a circumstance which led the latter,
when he took up his abode in town in 1778, to
quarter himself upon his old associate. It must
have been at No. 100 that Fuseli produced his
extraordinary " Nightmare," of which the success may be measured by the fact that it produced some five hundred pounds to its publisher
and some twenty to its inventor. In No. 100,
too, he painted his " Œdipus and his Daugh-
ters," and planned that Cyclopean enterprise,
the illustrated Shakespeare of Boydell. Thackeray thought poorly of that " black and ghastly
gallery," whose vast atlas folios spelled ruin to
the worthy alderman ; and a generation accustomed to the accomplished and instructed con-
ceptions of Mr. Edwin Abbey is hardly likely

to sympathise greatly with the murky Lears
and Macbeths of Fuseli, or even with his
" Titania "—for all that Allan Cunningham com-
pares it with Hogarth's " Strolling Actresses," a
comparison which, in this connection, has a
knell of condemnation.   One wonders whether
it was from St. Martin's Lane that Fuseli was
summoned by Horace Walpole to try his hand
at Dryden's Theodore and Honoria—a task
surely more in the line of Horace's friend, Lady
Di Beauclerk, who did the sublime studies " in
soot water " for the " Mysterious Mother."[1]
But in St. Martin's Lane Fuseli continued to
reside until 1788, when he married his model,
Miss Sophia Rawlins, of Bath, and moved to
72, Queen Anne Street, Cavendish Square.

In 1828, and, indeed, for at least a quarter of
a century afterwards, No. 96 was a colour-shop,
which, in Cunningham's " Handbook " of 1849
and 1850, the attentive reader is invited to " observe."   Its tenant previous to 1828 was one
Powell, whose mother for many years had made
" a pipe of wine" from a vine nearly a hundred feet
long which was attached to the establishment,
and which must have been much more remarkable than the historical plant in Bolt Court,

[1] As a matter of fact, Lady Di did illustrate Dryden's
" Fables " in 1797, with Bartolozzi for her engraver.

from which, in 1784, Dr. Johnson gathered "three bunches of grapes." In Powell's time, No. 96 was a fine old building whose Queen Anne door-frame was deeply carved with foliage and flowers after the fashion of the doorways in Great Ormond Street; and, like Thornhill's house, it had a painted staircase. This, which represented figures viewing a procession, had been executed about 1732 by a French decorator named Clermont for the notorious empiric, Dr. Misaubin, to whom, either ironically or in good faith, Fielding inscribed his version of Molière's "Médecin malgré lui," known as the "Mock Doctor." John Misaubin was the son of a French pastor in Spitalfields, and, if we are to take Fielding seriously, a man of parts and hospitality. "I'd send for Misaubin, and take his pill," says Bramston's "Man of Taste"; and, no doubt, a good many "men of taste" knocked at the Doctor's Queen Anne portal in the Lane. The learned and platitudinous Dr. Trusler, who was briefed by Mrs. Hogarth, affirms that the "meagre figure" in Plate V of the "Harlot's Progress" is "Dr. Miʒebank, a foreigner." If so, he cannot, as contended by other commentators, also be the bow-legged dwarf who is wiping his spectacles in the third picture of "Marriage *A-la-Mode*."

But seeing that Misaubin died in 1734, it is quite possible that the scene of the Quack Doctor in Hogarth's masterpiece is laid at No. 96 ; and as he had an Irish wife, it is also possible that in the fierce virago with the hoop, " spread out "—as Hazlitt says—" like a turkey-cock's feathers," he was thinking of the Misaubin establishment.[1] The doctor made a considerable fortune by his nostrums, a fortune which his grandson, after the manner of Hogarth's Rake, promptly squandered, ending his days in brief space, not in Bedlam, but in St. Martin's Workhouse.

Close upon No. 96, and turning to the left, came Cecil Court, a somewhat different place from the reputable paved passage, flanked with tall "mansions," which now leads from St. Martin's Lane to Charing Cross Road. It was in Cecil Court that Hogarth's mother, a ma-

[1] Whether the furniture and accessories of M. de la Pilule's consulting-room were accurate studies from those of Misaubin, it is of course difficult to affirm. But as an instance of the care with which Hogarth wrought out the details of his picture-dramas, there is now in the National Gallery a carefully finished pencil and stump study by him of a skull, which, though reversed, closely resembles that which stands on the quack's table. Hogarth has added the marks on the cranium, and apparently by an afterthought, has exaggerated the posterior part.

jestic old lady, lived and died, her death being
thus chronicled by the " Gentleman's Magazine " : " [June] 11 [1735] Mrs. *Hogarth*,
Mother of the celebrated Mr. *Hogarth*, of a
Fright occasioned by the Fire." This con-
flagration, which took place on the 9th, must
have been an event for Cecil Court, and was
alleged to have been lighted by a certain brandy-
selling Mrs. Calloway, who having been served
by her landlord with a notice to quit, determined
in revenge to " warm all her rascally neighbours," a resolution which she carried out in a
very effective and business-like manner. No
fewer than fourteen houses were burned, and
one belonging to John Huggins, Esq., late
Warden of The Fleet, was " greatly damaged."
For " John Huggins', Esquire," co-criminal
with the infamous Bambridge of an earlier
paper,[1] there is little need of pity ; but if it is to be
inferred that his residence was in the Court itself,
it seems clear that the houses must have been
of a superior class. Another resident in later
years was the father of Wilkie's engraver, Abra-
ham Raimbach ; and in Cecil Court, as already
stated in " An English Engraver in Paris,"[2]
Raimbach himself was born. History has,

[1] See *Post*, " A Paladin of Philanthropy."
[2] See " Miscellanies," First Series, p. 145.

however, recorded no other notable dwellers in
Cecil Court, while concerning the next Court,
St. Martin's, it is silent altogether.[1] By this
time (1901) the northwestern side of St. Martin's Court has been pulled down, and those
who seek to recognise in it the "large handsome Court" of Strype with the "good new-
built Houses" and "open Square in the
Midst" must be endowed with exceptional
powers of mental reconstruction. North of
St. Martin's Court there are but two sites
which concern this paper. One, where the
Westminster County Court now stands, is that
of the tavern known as New or Young Slaughter's ; the other, which must have been at the
entrance to Cranbourn Street, was occupied by
the more famous Old Slaughter's. In a house
between these two lodged, from 1720 to 1725,
that favourite of Addison and Steele, and laugh-
ing-stock of Pope and Gay, Ambrose Philips.
" Pastoral Philips," in spite of what Swift

---

[1] This latter statement is inexact, for, as we have ascertained since the present paper was first penned, it was
at the Charing Cross Road end of St. Martin's Court (not
Lane) that once stood the ham-and-beef shop to which
Lamb's wandering thoughts reverted on Skiddaw.
Thackeray also mentions it in his powerful story of the
murderess Catherine Hayes (*Fraser's Magazine,* 1839–40).

called his "little flams on Miss Carteret," has
never ranked as a great poetical name, even
among the easy eminences of the Georgian era ;
and certainly to have enriched the language with
the epithet " namby-pamby," is scarcely the
crown which a self-respecting bard should
claim of Melpomene. Yet it is difficult not
to remember that it was to see Anne Oldfield
as Andromache in Philips' " borrowed play "
of the " Distrest Mother " that Sir Roger de
Coverley went in state to Drury Lane Playhouse—a fictitious fact of far greater moment
than the unquestioned and unvarnished truth
that John Kemble, long afterwards, acted its
Orestes in a costume borrowed from the illustrious Talma. And though the sham eclogue
which Gay laughed away in the " Shepherd's Week," is to-day only a little more forgotten than the "Shepherd's Week "itself, the
" Persian Tales " which honest Philips did into
English from Pétis de La Croix were long
among the popular stock of pedlars, and the
delight, after M. Antoine Galland's " Arabian
Nights," of generations of schoolboys. One
cannot feel wholly ungrateful to the harmless
verseman whose highest ambition went no
higher—in his arch-tormentor's words—than :—

" To wear red stockings, and to dine with STEELE."

But Ambrose Philips and his red stockings have broken the logical order of our progression, an accident which may perhaps justify the farther divergence of referring to Old Slaughter's coffee-house before speaking of its rival and successor, Young Slaughter's. Previous to 1842, when it was pulled down to make room for the prolongation of Cranbourn Street, Old Slaughter's stood close to the southern corner of Great Newport Street, and its number in the Lane was 75.[1] From a sketch made by Mr. F. W. Fairholt in 1826, it must then have been a comfortable building with bow windows which looked down Long Acre. It dated as far back as 1692, when it was started by the Thomas Slaughter from whom it derived its name,

[1] In Kelly's first street Directory for 1841, No. 75 is given as "Reid and Co., Old Slaughter's Coffee-house." In 1842, No. 75 has disappeared altogether. Five or six years later Thackeray revived its bygone memory in "Vanity Fair." For it is from "the Old Slaughter's Coffee-house," on the 10th April, 1815, that George Osborne sets out, in a blue coat with brass buttons, and a neat buff waistcoat, to marry Amelia Sedley; and it is at the same caravanserai, ten years later, that John the waiter tells Major William Dobbin, *sans rancune*, how the late Captain Osborne had died in his debt. "He owes me three pound at this minute," says John of the Slaughter's, and he wonders whether George's old father would ever pay the money.

and who kept it for more than seven-and-forty
years. Dryden was reported to have frequented
it in early days, and Pope. But its regular
customers were the artist-folk of the Lane and
its vicinity. Hither from Leicester Fields would
come Hogarth, bragging of the new-old theories
in the " Analysis," and scoffing at the " grand
contorno " of the *virtuosi;* hither Hayman, and
the gold-chaser Moser, and Isaac Ware, the
chimney-sweep-turned-architect who translated
" Palladio " ; and (from his studio over the way)
Roubillac, raving in broken English of the beauties of the Chevalier Bernini. Here, again, would
be seen the shrewd Swiss enameller Rouquet, taking notes of the state of the Arts in England for the
benefit of Marshal Belle-Isle ; and Gravelot,
who held that no Englishman could draw ; and
" Friar " John Pine of the incised " Horace,"
who had a print-shop at No. 88. Luke Sulli-
van, the engraver of the " March to Finchley,"
McArdell the mezzo-tinter, and Richard Wilson from Covent Garden were also well-known
visitors ; while in later days, when evening
drew on, and the last rays of light faded from
the unfinished canvas, the tall ungainly figure
of David Wilkie would slip in quietly to a remote table and a hurried meal, at which modest
repast he would sometimes be joined by a

noisier and more demonstrative companion, the Benjamin Robert Haydon, whose ambitious "Curtius leaping into the Gulf" now adorns a London Restaurant.[1] Nor was there wanting a sprinkling of authors to carry on the traditions of Pope and Dryden, for Collins of the "Odes" is reported to have used this time-honoured hostelry, and Goldsmith refers to its Orators in the "Essays" as if his knowledge was experimental. Here, too (as everywhere), was to be found Johnson, studying spoken French from the mouths of the French frequenters of the place, and (as always) expressing his opinions in forcible language. The "fasting Monsieurs"—so he styles them in his "London"—disgusted him with their hare-brained and irresponsible frivolity. "For anything I see," he declared, confirming the previous verdict of a friend, "foreigners are Fools!"

As already stated, Old Slaughter's came to an end in 1842, being then one hundred and fifty years old. It had attained the mature age of sixty-seven summers before its rival at No. 82, New or Young Slaughter's, came into existence —an existence brief in comparison and relatively undistinguished. Young Slaughter's legend

[1] Messrs. Gatti's in Villiers Street, Strand.

seems limited to the fact that, *circa* 1765, Smeaton, Solander, Banks, John Hunter, Captain Cook, and certain other scientific or literary men, used it for Club meetings. Upper St. Martin's Lane, as the part north of Long Acre is called, is barren of memories—at all events in the eighteenth century. But over-against Old Slaughter's on the east side was No. 70, where, in 1775 Nathaniel Hone, among other specimen's of his skill, exhibited that irreverent picture of Sir Joshua as " The Pictorial Conjuror displaying the whole Art of Optical Deception," a composition, which in its first form, had the supplementary discredit of insulting Angelica Kauffman. Below No. 70, at No. 63, was the entrance to the studio in which Roubillac took refuge after he had quitted Peter's Court, and from which, in 1762, he was buried in St. Martin's churchyard, his successor being his pupil, Nicholas Read, proficient in " pancake clouds," whose chief claim to remembrance lies in the tradition that he worked upon the shrouded figure of Death in Roubillac's monument to Mr. Nightingale and his wife in Westminster Abbey. After these the east side becomes uninteresting, except for the residence at No. 60 of Thomas Chippendale, " Upholder," whose name is probably better known now than in his own day,

though we still seem to be ignorant of the dates
of his birth and death.   It was from his St.
Martin's Lane shop, in 1754, that he put forth
his "Gentleman and Cabinet-Maker's Director,"
a sumptuous series of one hundred and sixty
copper-plates dedicated to the Earl of Northumberland, and even now not entirely eclipsed by
the severer designs of Thomas Sheraton.   Some
of the courts and side streets may detain us for
a moment.   In New Street was the " Golden
Head," from which in 1770, young Flaxman
sent a modest " Portrait of a Gentleman " as
his first contribution to the Academy ; and it
was at the " Pine Apple " in the same street
that Johnson, on coming to town, was wont to
seek refreshment.   " I dined (said he) very well
for eightpence, with very good company. . . .
Several of them had travelled.   They expected
to meet every day ; but did not know one another's names.   It used to cost the rest a shilling, for they drank wine; but I had a cut of
meat for sixpence, and bread for a penny, and
gave the waiter a penny ; so that I was quite
well served, nay, better than the rest, for they
gave the waiter nothing."   In May's Buildings
(where in later years the club called The Eccen-
trics held its sittings) there flourished, according to Foote's " Taste," a manufactory of sham

Rembrandts and Ostades which deceived the opulent amateur and filled the pockets of the Puffs and Carmines of the day. Probably it was the east side of the old thoroughfare which most merited the title we have borrowed from Allan Cunningham to head these desultory memoranda. If they are here brought to a close, it is by no means because the subject is exhausted, for opposite to the church, and not far from the turnpike referred to at the beginning of this paper, stood the Watch or Round-House, an institution which should assuredly be fruitful of anecdote. But even in topography one must draw the line somewhere, and we draw it at this popular resort of the Georgian nobility and gentry. *" Le secret d'ennuyer est celui de tout dire."*

A PALADIN OF PHILANTHROPY.

IN February, 1785, when the books of the "late learned Samuel Johnson, Esq.; LL.D. Deceased," were being sold by Mr. Christie at his Great Room in Pall Mall, one of the persons present was the poet, Samuel Rogers, then a youth of two-and-twenty. He recalls his attendance at this particular sale in order to chronicle the fact that he there met a very old gentleman,—so old that the flesh of his face looked like parchment,—who entertained the younger generation of Mr. Christie's clients by discoursing of the changes that had taken place in London within a memory which, to his auditors, seemed to rival that of the Count de St. Germain. He himself who spoke, he asserted, had "shot snipes in Conduit-Street," when Conduit Street was an open mead; and it may be added that he had a friend, Mr. Carew Hervey Mildmay, who had done likewise.[1] Concerning his age, beyond these indications,

[1] Mr. Mildmay died in 1780, being then ninety-six. Fifty years ago people were wont to boast of shooting snipe—it is always snipe!—on the marshy site of Belgravia (the Five Fields); now they speak of Battersea and Bedford Park.

he was reticent; and he was popularly supposed to be what he appeared to be—at least a hundred. Oddly enough, the only well-known portrait of him was taken by Samuel Ireland at just this time and place. It exhibits a very ancient personage indeed, lean as a grasshopper, with a profile not unlike that of Fielding in Hogarth's posthumous sketch. He wears a military-looking hat, and a caped coat with deep cuffs and ruffles. His sword-hilt projects between his skirts; and in his right hand, which is propped upon a stout walking-cane, he holds a book which has been knocked down to him, and which he is reading attentively without the aid of spectacles.

The cadet of a Jacobite family in the West Riding of Yorkshire, with an English father and an Irish mother, General JAMES EDWARD OGLETHORPE—for such was the name of Ireland's sitter—was not so old as he looked, and perhaps wished to be thought. When in July, 1785, he died, contemporary prints vaguely stated his age at one hundred and two,[1] and his epitaph in Cran-

---

[1] " ONE HUNDRED Two! Mathusalem in age,
A vigorous soldier, and a virtuous sage :
He founded GEORGIA, gave it laws and trade;
He saw it flourish, and he saw it fade ! "

ham Church—an incontinent production by Capel Lofft which rivals the performances of Pope's Dr. Freind—is silent as to the date of his birth. His fullest biographer, Mr. Wright, and his latest biographer, Mr. Bruce, concur in fixing this as June 1, 1689. But shortly after Mr. Wright's book appeared in 1867, an indefatigable amateur of the parish register, the late Col. J. L. Chester, pointed out in " Notes and Queries " that the date of the General's birth was plainly recorded at St. Martin's-in-the-Fields, being there given as December 22, 1696—a date which (as regards day and month) is practically confirmed by the fact that, in the colony of Georgia, which he founded, the 21st December was long kept as his birthday. The seven years thus deducted from his lifetime make legend of many of the facts related of his youth. Even if he were really, as his epitaph avers, a " Captain-Lieutenant " of the Queen's Guards in 1714 (at eighteen), it is very improbable that he could have been the " Adjutant-General Oglethorpe " who, in the same year, travelled from Lyons to Turin with Dr. Berkeley. But it is pretty clear that in 1714 he matriculated at Corpus, where he was a Gentleman Commoner. In 1715, either upon the recommendation of Marlborough or Argyll, he took service under Prince Eugene, and assisted at the siege of Belgrade by the Austrians. For this we have his own authority. " Pray, General," said Johnson to him in 1772, " give us an account of the siege of Belgrade " (Boswell, by a slip of the pen, says Bender). Whereupon the old warrior, across the walnuts, and with the aid of some of the wine, described that military exploit. *Hac ibat Simois ; hic est Sigeia tellus.* " Here we were, here were the Turks," etc., etc., to all of which the Doctor " listened with the closest attention." It is from Boswell again, and indeed upon the same occasion, that we get the only other authentic anecdote of Oglethorpe's youth. *A propos* of duelling, Boswell tells the following story, as the General told it. Sitting once at table, under Eugene, with a certain Prince of Wurtemberg, the latter, by fillipping the surface of his wine, made some of it fly over the young volunteer, who was thus placed in the awkward dilemma of having to choose between accepting or resenting a gratuitous affront. Oglethorpe's resolution was quickly taken. Saying with a smile, "That's a good joke, but we do it much better in England ! " he raised his glass, and flung the contents in His Serenity's face. Whereupon an old General present pacifically observed, " *Il a bien fait, mon*

Prince, vous l'avez commencé," and the affair passed off in good humour.

With the peace of Passarowitz in 1718, hostilities between the Sultan and Charles VI were brought to a close, and with those hostilities ended Oglethorpe's experiences as a Continental volunteer. A year or two later, by the death of his second brother, Sir Theophilus Oglethorpe, he succeeded to the family estate of Westbrook, near Godalming, which included a mansion where the Pretender was reported to have lain in hiding; and in October, 1722, like his father and brother before him, he took his seat in Parliament for Haslemere. As a senator, he was conspicuous for a frank speech and a benevolent motive. Colonisation, commerce, free trade, and the silk manufacture in England were things which interested him ; and he had a knack of homely illustration which was by no means ineffective in debate. But he was a working rather than a talking politician, and his most valuable Parliamentary efforts were in connection with the Committee of 1729-30 into the state of the debtors' prisons in London—a Committee which, indeed, had originated with himself. A friend of his own, one Robert Castell, an amiable amateur architect, who, under guise of an introduction to Vitruvius, had prepared, and dedicated to Richard, Earl of Burlington, a stately subscription *folio* on the Villas of the Ancients, subsequently—and perhaps consequently—fell into grave pecuniary difficulties. He was thrown into the Fleet, at that time farmed by a wretch named Thomas Bambridge, who, in his capacity of Warden, cleared some five thousand pounds a year by fleecing and oppressing the unfortunate debtors under his charge. As long as Castell could contrive to pay heavily for the privilege of residing in one of the four or five shabby streets which then constituted the Rules or Liberties, he was permitted to do so. But when he became unable to satisfy the Warden's immoderate demands for "presents" (as they were called), he was mercilessly transferred to one of the three spunging houses[1] attached to the prison, a crowded and loathsome den in which, moreover, the smallpox was then raging. He had never (as he protested) had that distemper; was extremely apprehensive of it; caught it almost immediately; and died in a few days, de-

[1] Johnson (whose knowledge was experimental) accurately defined these establishments in the "Dictionary" as houses "to which debtors are taken before commitment to prison, where *the bailiffs sponge upon them, and riot at their cost.*"

claring, with his last breath, that he had been murdered by Bambridge. Oglethorpe promptly brought his friend's deplorable fate to the notice of the House of Commons ; and a Select Committee to inquire into the state of the Gaols of the Kingdom was forthwith appointed, of which he was nominated Chairman. Its three Reports on the Fleet and the King's Bench prisons, still to be read in volume eight of Cobbett's " Parliamentary History," disclose the most sickening story of barbarity, extortion, and insanitation. The good and the bad, the sick and the hale, were found to be herded together in filthy dungeons ; deaths, often from sheer starvation, were of daily occurrence ; iron collars, thumbscrews, and the heaviest fetters were freely used for the refractory ; and an unfortunate prisoner might be subjected to all this for the paltry debt of a shilling, which became the nucleus of endless gratuities and " considerations," and the pretext for perpetual confinement. As a result of the labours of Oglethorpe's committee some of the more crying of these abuses were remedied ; but many yet remained, thirty years later, to arouse the pious horror of John Howard. The " garnish " money of the " Beggar's Opera " and the " begging box " of the " Citizen of the World " still swelled the profits of the Deputy-Marshal and his myrmidons; the terrible gaol-fever continued to claim its tribute of victims; and the prison interiors of Goldsmith's " Vicar " and Fielding's " Amelia " can scarcely be regarded as evidences of an attained ideal. One of the most interesting mementoes of Oglethorpe's endeavours—which, by the way, were not restricted to his Parliamentary labours —is Hogarth's picture, now in the National Portrait Gallery, of Bambridge under examination. It was painted for Sir Archibald Grant of Monymusk, Knight of the Shire for Aberdeen, and a member of the Committee. [1] Horace Walpole, who had the original oil-sketch, is loud in appreciation of the rendering of the inhuman gaoler. " It is the very figure that Salvator Rosa would have drawn for Iago in the moment of detection. Villainy, fear, and conscience are mixed in yellow and livid on his countenance, his lips are contracted by tremor, his face advances as eager to lie, his legs step back as thinking to make his escape ; one hand is thrust precipitately into his bosom, the fingers of the other are catching uncertainly at his button-holes. If this was a portrait [and it was],

[1] Sir James Thornhill, the painter, who probably got Hogarth the commission, was also on the Committee.

it is the most speaking that ever was drawn ; if it was not, it is still finer." [1]

The Committee of Enquiry into the state of the Gaols was not Oglethorpe's first philanthropic essay. In 1728 he had published anonymously a little pamphlet entitled " The Sailor's Advocate," in which he exposed the abuses of the cruel method of impressment countenanced by the Admiralty of his day, and, indeed, of many a day to follow. But the insight he had gained into the horrors of prison discipline had now turned his thoughts definitely in fresh directions ; and he began to cast about to find employment and a future for those hapless beings who, from no unpardonable fault of their own, were most liable to fall into the clutches of Bambridge and his kind. After prolonged and anxious consideration, he was led to believe that the true solution of the question must be sought in assisted emigration—a conclusion in which he was fortified (he says) by the successful settlement of Derry (under James I) by the Corporation of London. The district he selected for his field of operation was one which had already attracted the projector. It lay on the east coast of North

[1] This sketch is now (1901) in the possession of Mr. Fairfax Murray.

America, beyond and below the Savannah River, and to the north of the Spanish territory of Florida. The Spaniards, who claimed all America, threatened it periodically from the south; bands of desperate runaway blacks infested it from the Carolinas; and to the west were dense and trackless woods, filled with Cherokees, Chickasaws, and other hostile and predatory Indian tribes. But Oglethorpe, nothing daunted, put forward his scheme. With twenty other trustees, he petitioned the Throne for an Act of Incorporation, and in June, 1732, obtained a charter for settling and establishing a new colony, to be called Georgia, in honour of George II. In a couple of pamphlets, published in the same year, and entitled respectively "An Essay on Plantations," and "A New and Accurate Account of the Provinces of South Carolina and Georgia," he developed his ideas, which he affirmed to be "the result of various readings and conversations in many years." His appeal was warmly responded to by the public, and Parliament handed over to the trustees a sum of £10,000, the residue of a grant voted but not paid to Berkeley for his frustrate college in the Bermudas. The trustees, who were themselves large contributors to the scheme, were, by their Charter, restrained from receiving any salary, fee, perquisite or profit whatsoever, nor could they hold any land ; conditions entirely honourable to themselves, and not subsequently discredited. Slavery, which prevailed in the Carolinas, was also strictly prohibited, eventually by special Statute. After careful inquiries, thirty-five families, comprising representatives of many trades, and numbering in all one hundred and twenty persons, were chosen for the first settlers ; and on the 16th of November, 1732, they set sail from Gravesend in the " Anne " (Captain Thomas). They were accompanied by Oglethorpe himself ; by a chaplain, the Rev. Henry Herbert, and by a Piedmontese named Amatis, whose function it was to instruct the new colonists in the art of rearing silkworms and winding silk. Oglethorpe who was empowered to act as a Colonial Governor, was at this date six-and-thirty, and notwithstanding an undeniable touch of romance in his character, still unmarried. He had already shown energy and tenacity of purpose ; he was now to exhibit, in fuller measure, his gifts as an organiser and administrator. He is described as tall, manly, and very handsome ; as dignified, but not austere ; and if it be added to these things that, as a country gentleman, he had an ample fortune, which he freely employed in the furtherance of his charitable designs, may fairly claim to be written, like Abou Ben Adhem, " as one that loved his fellow-men."

On January 13, 1733, after a prosperous voyage of some sixty days, the "Anne" dropped anchor outside Charleston Bar in South Carolina, and Oglethorpe proceeded to select the site of the new settlement. The spot he fixed upon was a flat bluff or headland on the right (or south) bank of the Savannah, where, about ten miles from the mouth, it bends eastward to the Atlantic. This site extended from five to six miles into the country, with a river frontage of a mile. Forthwith the clearing of the ground began, and streets and squares were marked out. By the middle of March five houses were built or building, and a crane and magazines had been erected. The settlers had been solemnly warned against the dangers of drunkenness; and friendly relations were already in progress with the nearest body of Indians, a branch of the Creek tribe, barely half a mile off, at Yamacraw. Oglethorpe's management of the Indians deserves the highest praise, and he speedily inspired them with a confidence which they never lost. They are "desirous," he wrote to the trustees, "to be subjects to his Majesty, King George, to have lands given them among us, and to breed their children at our schools. Their chief, and his beloved man, who is the second man in the nation, desire to be instructed in the Christian religion." A month or two later a formal convention was concluded with the Indians, under which the country between the Savannah and the Altamaha (Goldsmith's " wild Altama " in " The Deserted Village "), as far as the tide waters flowed, and including most of the islands, was ceded to the trustees ; and, by a subsequent treaty, the Creeks engaged to have no dealings with the Spaniards or the French. As a protection against the former, Oglethorpe erected a strong outpost on the Ogechee river, which he christened (in honour of his patron) Fort Argyll; and this was followed, not long after, by the creation, on St. Simon's Island, at the mouth of the Altamaha, of the settlement and military station of Frederica. Meanwhile new emigrants continued to reach Savannah. A large body of these were Protestants, from Salzburg, whose expulsion from their native land, by episcopal edict, had excited considerable sympathy in England.[1] Oglethorpe and his trustees invited them to Georgia, where, in March,

[1] The Exodus of the Salzburgers has been made the subject of a picture by the German artist, Adolph Menzel.

1734, they arrived, to be welcomed warmly by the English colonists, and regaled, *inter alia*, with "very fine, wholesome English beer."[1] They took up their abode in a locality chosen for them by Oglethorpe's aid, which they named "Ebenezer." As soon as they were established there, Oglethorpe, leaving his new colony in the charge of a bailiff or storekeeper, named Causton, set sail for England in H. M. S. "Aldborough," taking with him his now firm friend, the old Creek chief or Mico, Tomo-Chichi, his wife, Senauki, his boy-nephew and successor, Tooanahowi, and Hillispilli, his war-captain.[2] Oglethorpe's politic object in choosing these traveling companions was to impress his Indian allies with the resources of Great Britain, and the importance of her institutions.

Tomo-Chichi and his suite had certainly a flattering reception in London. The war-cap-

[1] This very minor detail is mentioned for the sake of showing that Oglethorpe's objection to alcohol stopped at "fire-water." He would have been thoroughly in sympathy with the respective lessons of Hogarth's "Beer Street" and "Gin Lane."

[2] Tomo-Chichi in his furs, and Tooanahowi holding a live eagle, were painted in London by William Verelst. It was a different Verelst who, in 1710, had painted the Four Iroquois Indian Kings of the *Spectator*.

tain having been with difficulty restrained from appearing in his " native nothingness " of paint and feathers, the party were taken to Kensington in three coaches to interview George II, who received them very graciously, and allowed them £20 a week during their four months' stay in town. They subsequently visited the venerable Archbishop of Canterbury (Dr. William Wake) at Lambeth, and were made acquainted with whatever was " curious and worthy Observation in and about the Cities of *London* and *Westminster*." They received some £400 worth of presents, including a gold watch which was presented to Tooanahowi, with a pious admonition, by the youthful Duke of Cumberland. In return, they seem to have greatly (or gratefully) admired His Royal Highness's " Exercise of riding the manag'd Horse," and to have been specially impressed by the magnificence of the Life Guards and the glories of the Thames on Lord Mayor's Day. After their return to Georgia in October, some of the tribe sent an elaborate letter of thanks to Tomo-Chichi's English entertainers, but scarcely in a shape adapted for preservation in an autograph book. It consisted of the dressed skin of a young buffalo, painted by a Cherokee chief with red and black hieroglyphics; and in this form it long ornamented the Georgia Office in Old Palace Yard. Oglethorpe himself was also naturally the object of much attention, and he received many testimonies to the popularity of his enterprise. Some of these took peculiar forms. At the end of 1735 a certain eccentric Mr. Robert North, of Scarborough, offered prizes to the "Gentleman's Magazine" for the four best poems entitled "The Christian Hero" (the name, it will be remembered, of an early devotional manual by Captain Richard Steele of the Guards). The first prize was to be a gold medal with Oglethorpe's head on one side, and that of Lady Elizabeth Hastings (Steele's "Aspasia") on the other. Lady Elizabeth's effigy was, however, withheld at her own request, and that of Oglethorpe did not prove complimentary as a portrait. As for the poems —well, the poems may still be read in Sylvanus Urban his sixth volume. But the metrical utterance that really handed down Oglethorpe's name to posterity made its appearance a year later (1737). The couplet —

> "One, driv'n by strong Benevolence of Soul,
> Shall fly, like *Oglethorp*, from Pole to Pole —"

in ALEXANDER POPE'S epistle to Colonel Cotterell, has done more to preserve the memory of the founder of Georgia than all the records of the Office at Westminster.

During Oglethorpe's stay in England he had been actively promoting the interests of the new province, but beyond the fact that, from his seat in the House, he had warmly supported two Acts prohibiting the introduction into the settlement of spirits and slavery, his doings have not been particularly recorded. In December, 1735, he set out on his return voyage with two vessels, the "Symond" and the "London Merchant," having on board two hundred and twenty chosen settlers, and a fresh consignment of Salzburgers. He was accompanied, as missionaries, by John Wesley, at this time two-and-thirty, and his younger brother Charles, who was twenty-six. After a passage of many vexations and delays (like Fielding later, they were detained several weeks at the Isle of Wight by contrary winds), they reached their destination. Of course there were disappointments. Tybee Island, at the river-mouth, which should have been lighted, was still dark. But Savannah itself had greatly prospered in its founder's absence. Where, three years before, there had been only the "matted woods" of Goldsmith, now rose some two hundred comfortable dwellings with garden- and orchard-plots, and pasture lands filled with grazing cattle. There were even public recreation grounds, delightfully situated by the riverside, where flourished orange trees and tulip-laurels, and white mulberries for the silkworms, and tropical plants—coffee and cotton and *palma Christi*—which had been sent from the West Indies by Sir Hans Sloane. Savannah, however, was no longer to be Oglethorpe's chief care. The Spaniards, who had a stronghold at St. Augustine, in Florida, had begun to demonstrate uneasily along the Altamaha, and he turned his energies for the future mainly to the protection of the Southern frontier. A body of Gaelic Highlanders from Inverness were already installed at Darien, about twelve miles up the Altamaha ; and after adjusting some difficulties of the Salzburgers, who were dissatisfied with the site of Ebenezer, he hastened southward to St. Simon's Island at the river mouth. Here in brief space he established, and stocked with emigrants, the fort of Frederica, for many years to come the main bulwark against Spanish aggression in North America ; and it is with this fort on St. Simon's Island that, during the remainder of his stay in Georgia, he was chiefly connected.

It has already been mentioned that Oglethorpe was accompanied on his return from England by

the Wesley brothers.   Their subsequent history
is one of the difficult passages of the Georgia
chronicle.   Charles, the younger, who, besides
being chaplain, was to be Oglethorpe's secretary,
appears to have speedily wearied of his lay duties,
added to which, during Oglethorpe's absence
from Frederica, he became involved in a tangle of
misunderstandings with the settlers — misunderstandings embittered by jealousies and complicated by feminine tittle-tattle.   In a very few
weeks he found Frederica too hot for him ("I
was overjoyed at my deliverance out of this
furnace"), and not long afterwards resigned his
post, parting kindly with Oglethorpe, who, in
spite of his impetuosity, never bore malice.
Meanwhile his elder brother, whom Oglethorpe
liked less, was not prospering at Savannah.   He
had come out to convert the Indians, but he
never learned their language.   On the other
hand, he seems to have contrived to make himself exceedingly distasteful to the colonists.   At
this stage of his career — as he himself admitted
later — he was a bigoted High Churchman.
His exhortations, rigorous in doctrine and personal in tone, were angrily resented by the very
mixed community of the new settlement.   He
is, moreover, alleged to have "interfered in
family quarrels and the broils of social life."

Finally came the *affaire du cœur* which has been so frequently related. Always susceptible to feminine charm, he became attached to the storekeeper's niece, a designing coquette, who had nursed him through a fever, and deliberately laid herself out to attract him. Whether he actually made known his sentiments is obscure, but the Salzburg elders were certainly consulted privately as to the expediency of his marrying. They reported unfavourably, and the lady promptly consoled herself with a rival admirer. When afterwards, for some levity of behaviour as a married woman, Wesley declined to admit her to the Communion Table, her uncle and husband indicted him for defamation. The suit failed, but Savannah thenceforth became impossible for John Wesley, and he returned to England in December, 1737, as Whitefield was setting out to join him. Whitefield, in other ways, was equally ineffectual ; and he, also, made no long stay in Georgia. In no case does there seem to have been any actual rupture with Oglethorpe. But from a letter he wrote later, *à propos* of the excellent "Practice of Christianity" which the good Manx Bishop, Dr. Wilson, had drawn up at his request, "towards an Instruction for the Indians," he was manifestly of opinion that the teaching of "our

Methodists" (by which he must be understood to mean the brothers and their successor) had not proved to be adapted to the spiritual requirements of the colony. Probably he would personally have preferred more loving-kindness and a little less formality.

The Wesleys, however, are but an episode in Georgian history; and during their residence in the settlement can scarcely have had any prolonged intercourse with Oglethorpe, whose life henceforward reads like a realisation of the old stage direction, "excursions and alarms." Actually or indirectly he was continuously occupied in watching or checkmating the aggressive movements of the Spaniards; and his resources, offensive and defensive, were uncertain and inadequate. The Indians, his best friends, were excitable, and not always to be controlled by civilisation; the Carolinians, besides being committed to slave-labour, were self-seeking and obstructive; while the Salzburgers, though inoffensive enough in their "petrified Sabbath" at Ebenezer, declined to fight, even for hearth and home, and ultimately had to "fold their tents" altogether. After nine months of defending Georgia against its different dangers, Oglethorpe took advantage of a temporary lull to sail again for England, and beat up recruits. He was re-

ceived with renewed enthusiasm, not a little
heightened by the fact that the Court of
Madrid, while privately strengthening St.
Augustine, had the audacity to demand that
neither Oglethorpe nor his levies should be
allowed to go back. Nevertheless, with the
approval of Government, his regiment of 600
men was raised ; and in the following September
(1738), he once more reached St. Simon's with
the title of commander-in-chief of all his
Majesty's forces in Georgia and South Carolina.
Some further time was occupied in procuring
and concluding fresh treaties with the Indians ;
and then came the long deferred Declaration
of War with Spain, one of the first results of
which was that Oglethorpe was ordered to
reduce St. Augustine. This, a few months
later, he prepared to do, but not with his usual
good fortune. He had a fair equipment of
regulars, Carolina militia, and Indians, and this
land force, numbering some two thousand men,
was intended to be supported from the sea by
English men-of-war. But the Indians proved
unmanageable ; the colonial militia, besides
being inefficient, deserted freely ; and the fleet
failed to render the aid expected. Sickness
and disaffection complicated matters, and after
investing St. Augustine (which was found to be

strongly garrisoned and well defended) for five weeks, Oglethorpe had no option but to withdraw ingloriously, to the great prejudice of his prestige both abroad and at home, where his old patron, the Duke of Argyll, had to explain in the House of Lords (what was indeed the truth) that the enterprise had miscarried " only for want of supplies necessary to a possibility of success."

Fortunately, for nearly two years after the siege of St. Augustine, Spain remained comparatively quiet. Then, in the spring of 1742, came Oglethorpe's opportunity. Before he had been the attacker, now he was to be the attacked, and the story, on a smaller scale, has a dash of the Elizabethan days. With Castilian deliberation the Spaniards of Florida and the Havana fitted out a pompous armada of forty or fifty ships, snows, galleys, and periaguas, the purpose of which was to sweep the heretics, summarily and forever, from the North American settlements. The key of Georgia was St. Simon's Island, and St. Simon's Island, the defences of which had been recently strengthened, could not be neglected by an invader. Into St. Simon's Island Oglethorpe accordingly threw himself with a rapidly organised band of followers. When, after an unsuccessful attack on Fort

William (in Cumberland Island), the Spaniards arrived in St. Simon's Sound, he allowed them to land, spiked the guns of a smaller fort to the south, and retired upon Frederica, which was flanked by a dense oak forest, and approached by a morass. Here, under cover of the wood, and excellently served by his Indian scouts, he attacked the enemy in detail, a course which subjected them to much the same fate as that which befell Braddock's ill-starred expedition, fourteen years later, against Fort Duquesne. Notwithstanding their superiority, numbers of them, including several officers of distinction, were killed by sallies and ambuscades, and Oglethorpe himself, as a leader, seems to have shown not only extraordinary resource and decision, but also marked personal gallantry, taking two Spaniards prisoner, on one occasion, with his own hand. Finally, by a fortunate stratagem, he contrived, through the medium of a French spy, to persuade his foes that an English fleet was on its way to his relief—a statement which was opportunely supported by the chance appearance of some vessels off the coast. After about a week of this desultory and disastrous warfare, the discomfited Spanish forces re-embarked, with Oglethorpe at their heels. They made a renewed but fruitless attack upon

Fort William, which was bravely defended by
Ensign Stuart. In a few days more they had
faded away in the direction of St. Augustine,
and Oglethorpe was able to order a thanksgiving
for the end of the invasion. Seven or eight
hundred men had put to flight more than five
thousand ; and Whitefield might well write (as
he did) that " the deliverance of Georgia from
the Spaniards is such as cannot be paralleled but
by some instances out of the Old Testament."

During the remainder of his stay in Georgia,
Oglethorpe continued to " harass the Spaniard "
by all the means at his command. But he was
ill-supported from home both with money and
men ; and what was worse, his military operations had involved him personally in financial
difficulties which sooner or later must have
necessitated his return to England. The proxi-
mate cause of that return, however, was
apparently to meet certain charges which had
been preferred against him by one of his sub-
ordinates, Lieut.-Colonel Cook. In June, 1744,
these were declared by a Board of General Officers to be " false, malicious, and without founda-
tion," and Cook was summarily dismissed the
service. A month or two later (September 15) the
"Gentleman's Magazine" records the marriage
of " Gen. *Oglethorpe*,—to the only Daughter of

the late Sir *Nathan Wright*, Bt., of *Cranham Hall, Essex.*" The lady, who was thirty-five, brought him a fresh fortune (Georgia must by this time have absorbed his own), and a pleasant Jacobean country-house with an old-fashioned garden. One of Mr. Urban's poets seems to have expected that Mrs. Oglethorpe would henceforth share her husband's " fatigues, and conduct in the field." But Oglethorpe never again went back to Georgia, which was thenceforth left to go its own gait, and adopt slave labour. In the Forty-Five, he was appointed to a command under that corpulent rival of Eugene and Marlborough, " Billy the Butcher," who subsequently accused him of "lingering on the road " with his rangers in pursuit of the rebels. " Lingering" was not a fault of Oglethorpe, who was promptly acquitted by court-martial—the King confirming the verdict. But though he was later made a Lieutenant-General, this incident, coupled with some distrust of his Jacobite antecedents, practically closed his career as a soldier. For several years he continued to speak ably and earnestly in the House of Commons on matters military and philanthropic. Then, in 1754, two years after the trustees had finally washed their hands of Georgia, he lost the seat which he had held through seven Parliaments ; and in 1765, two years after Florida was transferred to England at the Treaty of Paris, he became a full General, soon to be the oldest in the British army. But it was twenty years more before he finally quitted the scene, living past the American Revolution and the famous Declaration which made Georgia independent, to die at last in his Essex home, not as one might suppose, of old age, but of a violent fever which would have killed him at any time. He is buried in the little church at Cranham, where his widow was ultimately laid beside him.

There are many references to Oglethorpe in the memoirs of his day, through which he flits fitfully for half a century, vigorous, bright-eyed, and too eager of speech to complete his sentences. He was familiar, of course, with Boswell, to which eminent "Authour," after the publication of the "Tour in Corsica," he introduced himself in a particularly gratifying manner. "My name, Sir, is Oglethorpe, and I wish to be acquainted with you." He bade him not marry till he had first put the Corsicans in a proper situation. "You may make a fortune in the doing of it," said he ; "or, if you do not, you will have acquired such a character as will entitle you to make a fortune "—words

which, if correctly reported, have a curious odd
suggestion of his own experience. He was
also known to Johnson, whose "London" he
had been one of the earliest to praise "in all
companies," and there can be no doubt that
such lines as those in that poem which speak of
"peaceful deserts, yet unclaimed by Spain,"
which might afford an asylum to the oppressed,
must have found a responsive echo in Oglethorpe's heart. Both the Doctor and Boswell
seem to have proposed to write their friend's
life, but neither did ; and we are left to explain
their neglect either by indolence, or that absence of effective biographical material and pre-
dominance of minor detail which have proved
such a stumbling-block to Oglethorpe's biographers. Another contemporary whom he knew
was Goldsmith, to whom he offered Cranham
as an asylum from the *fumum strepitumque
Romæ.* He sends him five pounds for a charitable purpose, and adds—"if a farm and a
mere country scene will be a little refreshment
from the smoke of London, we shall be glad of
the happiness of seeing you at Cranham Hall."
Whether Goldsmith went (he was familiar with
another Essex house, Lord Clare's at Gosfield),
is not related ; but it was when Oglethorpe was
calling upon him with Topham Beauclerk that

he was insulted by Pilkington's historical pound
—no, quarter-of-a-pound—of tea ; and it was at
Oglethorpe's, in April, 1773, that he sang Tony
Lumpkin's "Three Jolly Pigeons" and that
other ditty, to the tune of the "Humours of
Balamagairy" ("Ah, me ! when shall I marry
me !"), which was left out of "She Stoops"
because the "Miss Hardcastle" of the play
was no vocalist.   But the last, and perhaps the
most picturesque accounts of Oglethorpe are
given by Horace Walpole and Hannah More.
"I have got a new admirer," writes that lively
lady from Mrs. Garrick's in 1784.   "We flirt
together prodigiously ; it is the famous General
Oglethorpe, perhaps the most remarkable man
of his time . . . the finest figure you ever saw.
He perfectly realises all my ideas of Nestor.
His literature is great [he knew some of Miss
More's poetry by heart], his knowledge of the
world extensive, and his faculties as bright as
ever ; he is one of the three persons still living
who were mentioned by Pope ; Lord Mansfield
and Lord Marchmont are the other two. . . .
He is quite a *preux chevalier*, heroic, romantic,
and full of the old gallantry."   Walpole, who
was feebler, and frailer, and crippled with rheu-
matism, is hardly as enthusiastic as "St. Hannah," which was his own pet-name for Miss

More. But his report is fully confirmatory of Oglethorpe's young old age. " General Oglethorpe, who sometimes visits me . . . has the activity of youth when compared with me. His eyes, ears, articulation, limbs, and memory would suit a boy, if a boy could recollect a century backwards. His teeth are gone ; he is a shadow, and a wrinkled one ; but his spirits and his spirit are in full bloom ; two years and a half ago, he challenged a neighbouring gentleman for trespassing on his manor. '*I* could carry a cannon as easily as let off a pistol.'" And this was written in April, 1785, a month or two before Oglethorpe's death.

Hannah More's conventional " *preux chevalier* " strikes the final note of Oglethorpe better than her lightly-penned laudation. When he recommends her to study the old romances because it is the only way to acquire " noble sentiments," we are reminded not a little of his own kinship to Don Quixote ; when we read of his restless and impulsive energy, we recall (and the parallel was drawn in his own day) the ubiquitous exploits of Swift's Peterborough :

> " Mordanto gallops on alone,
> The roads are with his followers strown,
> This breaks a girth and that a bone ;

" His body active as his mind,
    Returning sound in limb and wind,
    Except some leather left behind."

He prosecuted Philanthropy in the spirit of a
Paladin, rejoicing in the obstacles, the en-
counters, the nights *sub Jove frigido ;* and it is
easy to imagine him declaiming to Johnson and
Goldsmith of the dangers of luxury, or quoting
the admirable precepts of Mr. Addison's
" Cato." His method, with all its advantages,
had demonstrable drawbacks ; and it is quite
possible that, reasoning with his heart rather
than his head, he was occasionally mistaken
both in the means he employed and the agents
he chose. It is possible, also, that in the presence of timidity or obstruction, he was sometimes imperious as well as impatient. *Nescit
cedere* was the motto of his family. But he
was a good man, disinterested, genuinely self-
denying, sincerely religious after his fashion,—a
fashion perhaps not altogether that of the Wesleys and Whitefields. In the matter of spirits
and slave labour he was plainly in advance of
his age ; and if he was not exactly (as Warton
claimed), " at once a great hero and a great
legislator," there can be no doubt as to his
" Benevolence of Soul," and his unfeigned sympathy with the oppressed. " His undertaking

will succeed," said the Governor of South Carolina, "for he nobly devotes all his powers to serve the poor and rescue them from their wretchedness." "He has taken care of us to the utmost of his ability," wrote the pastor of the grateful Salzburgers. "Others would not in many years have accomplished what he has brought about in one." And when, long after, the Spaniards sought to prejudice an Indian chief against his English friend, he answered, "We love him. It is true he does not give us silver; but he gives us everything we want that he has. He has given me the coat off his back and the blanket from under him."

THE STORY OF THE "SPECTATOR."

AMONG the items of intelligence in that un-rivalled confidential news-letter which Swift was in the habit of scribbling off periodically to Mrs. Dingley and Mrs. Johnson at Dublin, there are frequent references to the *Spectator* and its predecessor, the *Tatler*. In September, 1710, when the *Journal to Stella* commences, the *Tatler* had already reached its two hundred and nine-teenth number, and it must have been well-known to Swift's correspondents, since he speaks of it much as folks might speak of any paper that everybody is sure to see. Have they "smoakt" his letter (an admirable effort, by the way) concerning the corruptions of style ? It is greatly liked ; and he himself thinks it "a pure one." Next he is at work on a " poetical *Description of a Shower in London*,"[1] which he has finished—" all but the beginning." Why does " *Madam* Stell" persist that he wrote " Shaver " ?—he asks later. Elsewhere comes a reference to his share in Addison's *Adventures of a Shilling*,[2] the original hint for which the

[1] *Tatler*, No. 238.　　[2] *Tatler*, No. 249.

writer admits was given to him by a friend with
"an inexhaustible Fund of Discourse." Then
again we learn that Swift has drawn up, jointly
with Rowe and Prior, a protest against the
substitution of the words " Great Britain " for
" England," a proposal which is still under
debate.[1] A page or two farther on, the long-
pending misunderstanding with Steele has
reached an acute stage, and the record bears
witness to it. The *Tatlers* have fallen off; he
never sees either Addison or Steele ; he has
sent them no more hints. After this final
announcement (more deadly even than St. John's
Stamp Act!), one is prepared to hear of the
collapse of the paper. Oddly enough, it *does*
collapse in the very next entry. " *Steele's* last
Tatler came out to-day." " It was time, for he
grew cruel dull and dry." But Swift's love of
letters is greater than his irritation against his
alienated friends, and two months after, he is
writing enthusiastically of Steele's fresh venture.
" Have you seen the *Spectator* yet, a paper that
comes out every day ? 'Tis written by Mr.

[1] " In Scotland 35,000 signatures have been put to a
memorial asking that ' Great Britain ' and ' British ' should
be substituted for ' England ' and ' English ' in State
documents and official references to National institutions
like the Army " (*St. James's Gazette*, June 3, 1897).

Steele, who seems to have gathered new life, and have a new fund of wit ; it is in the same nature as his *Tatlers,* and they have all of them had something pretty." The praise was not undeserved. By March 16, 1711, when the above was written, the *Spectator* had been in vigorous existence for a fortnight. The short-faced sage was already taking the measure of mankind ; and if Sir Roger de Coverley had been but broadly outlined, the " Vision of Public Credit " had been penned, the story of Inkle and Yarico told, and Swift himself—though Mrs. Pilkington says he " had not laugh'd above twice " in his life—might reasonably have relaxed a little over the humours of Nicolini and the Lion. The *Spectator,* in short, had already become not merely an indispensable " Part of the Tea Equipage " (as claimed in its tenth issue), but a necessary of intellectual life. The smart young Templars (in their gorgeous dressing-gowns and strawberry sashes) were already crying out for it at Serle's and the Grecian ; it was permanently *en lecture* at Will's and the St. James's Coffee-house ; solemn quidnuncs and deliberate club-oracles (like Mr. Nisby of the *Citizen's Journal*) were beginning to take it for the text of their daily lucubrations ; while Mrs. Betty regularly carried it up at noon with Clarinda's dish of chocolate, between the newest patterns of Mr. Lutestring the mercer and the latest *poulet* from Mr. Froth.

The farewell number of the *Tatler* appeared on the 2d of January, 1711; the first number of the *Spectator* on the 1st of March following. In appearance the two papers were not dissimilar. Both were single *folio* leaves in double column; both—at all events when the *Tatler* was nearing its end—consisted of a solitary essay, headed by a Latin quotation and followed by a series of advertisements. Each was equally open to the charge, which had been made by an injured correspondent, of being offered to the world on "Tobacco Paper" in "Scurvy Letter." The only material difference was that the *Tatler* was published three times a week; and the *Spectator* was published daily, Sundays excepted, a difference scarcely enough in itself, one would suppose, to justify a fresh departure. But why the *Tatler* was prematurely concluded at the two hundred and seventy-first number, and the *Spectator* substituted for it, remains a problem the solution of which is still to seek. Steele's explanation is, that he had become individually identified with "Mr. Bickerstaff," and that this being so, his own fallible personality was powerless to give authority to

his office of Censor. "I shall not carry my
Humility so far as to call my self a vicious
Man, but at the same Time must confess, my
Life is at best but pardonable. And with no
greater Character than this, a Man would make
but an indifferent Progress in attacking prevail-
ing and fashionable Vices which Mr. *Bickerstaff* has done with a Freedom of Spirit that
would have lost both its Beauty and Efficacy,
had it been pretended to by Mr. Steele."
Upon the face of them these are sufficient
reasons, and they would have sufficed had it not
been for the fact that the *Tatler* was almost
immediately succeeded by another paper which
—as Swift says truly—was "in the same nature."
But it has also been suggested that there were
other reasons at which Steele himself, in his
valedictory words, hints vaguely. "What I
find is the least excusable Part of all this Work"
—he tells us—"is, that I have in some Places
in it touched upon Matters which concern both
the Church and State." This *obiter dictum*
opens too long and too perplexed an enquiry to
be here pursued in detail. Briefly stated, it
would seem that certain utterances of Mr.
Bickerstaff (not of necessity from Steele's pen)
had offended the Lord Treasurer, Harley, who
had come into power while the *Tatler* was in

progress, and that with those utterances its cessation was in some obscure way connected. A certain amount of colour is given to this contention in a tract by John Gay which expressly says that the *Tatler* was laid down as a sort of submission to, and composition with, the Government for some past offences. But here again it is to be observed that the *Spectator*, though, at the outset, professing neutrality between Whigs and Tories, neither observed nor engaged to observe a total abstinence from politics, so that, after all, caprice, or the weariness of the work which Swift alleges, may have played a foremost part in those "Thousand nameless Things" which made it irksome to Steele to continue to personate Mr. Isaac Bickerstaff. One circumstance, however, is beyond all question. Whether Defoe's *Review* or the *Athenian Mercury* or the *London Gazette* had most to do with the establishment of the *Tatler* may be debatable ; but there can be no doubt that the *Spectator* is the legitimate successor of the *Tatler*. The *Tatler* is the *Spectator* in the making ; and the *Spectator* is the developed and perfected *Tatler*, which, beginning with little save the *Quicquid agunt Homines* of its motto, gradually grew more ethical and less topical, restricting itself at last almost

exclusively to those separate essays on single
subjects which we are still wont to associate
with the name of the *Spectator*.

And if it can be proved that we owe the
Spectator to the *Tatler*, it is equally demonstrable that we owe Addison to Steele. When
that quondam trooper, "Christian Hero," and
stage-moralist, Queen Anne's Gazetteer, cast-
ing about for something to supplement an income which had always consisted largely of
expectations, hit upon the project of a paper
which should combine the latest Foreign Intelligence with the newest Gossip of the Town,
Addison was Secretary to the Lord-Lieutenant
of Ireland. At this date, his contributions to
literature consisted practically of an Opera of
Rosamond which had failed ; of a volume of
travels on the continent which (like Du Halde's
China) might have been written at home ; and
of the *Campaign*, a long-incubated[1] "Gazette
in *Rhyme*" concerning the Battle of Blenheim,
which included a fortunate simile about an angel
in a whirlwind. With Steele's literary venture
came Addison's literary opportunity. When, in

[1] "Next week will be Published the long expected
Poem, by Joseph Addison, Esq.: called The Campaign
and sold by Mr. Jacob Tonson" (*The Diverting Post,*
Dec. 2–9, 1704).

the new periodical which his old school-fellow's
inventive spirit had started, he recognised a re-
mark of his own, he sent him a contribution ;
and although it was some time before he began
to write regularly, it was clear from the first
that he had found a favourable vehicle for his
unique and hitherto latent gifts of humorous
observation. Steele's own qualifications were,
of course, by no means contemptible. He was
a sympathetic critic ; he had the true journalistic
faculty of taking fire readily ; his knowledge of
the contemporary theatre was not only exceptional but experimental ; and he had the keenest
eye for the ridiculous, the kindest heart for sor-
row and distress. But there can be little doubt
that in the finely-wrought La Bruyère-like
sketches of Tom Folio, Ned Softly, and the
Political Upholsterer, in the Rabelaisian
Frozen Voices and the delightful *Adventures of
a Shilling*, Addison at once attained a level
higher than anything at which his friend had
aimed. Re-acting upon Steele's own efforts,
these papers stimulated him to new ambitions,
and gave to the latter half of the *Tatler* as he
himself admitted, an elegance, a purity, and a
correctness which had been no initial part of his
hastily-conceived and hurriedly-executed scheme.
"I fared"—he said, in words which have

become historical—"like a distressed Prince who calls in a powerful Neighbour to his Aid ; I was undone by my Auxiliary; when I had once called him in, I could not subsist without Dependence on him." And whatever may be the secret history of the cessation of the *Tatler*, incapacity to carry it on can hardly be urged as an explanation. For, when it came to an end, not only had its original projector raised his own standard, but during the course of his enterprise, he had secured the services of an anonymous assistant whose equipment in the way of delicate irony and whimsical fancy has never yet been surpassed.

Under these auspices then, the *Spectator* made its first appearance on the 1st of March, 1711. Of the circumstances which preceded that appearance nothing definite has been recorded. Some outline, some scheme of campaign should—one would think—have been determined upon, before publication, but the information which has come down to us tends rather the other way. Tickell, who, ten years later, edited Addison's works with a strong bias in his deceased patron's favour, says, in apologising for including one of Steele's papers among Addison's, that "the Plan of the *Spectator*, as far as regards the feigned Person of the

Author, and of the several characters that compose his Club, was projected in concert with SIR RICHARD STEELE,"—a statement which some later critics have most unaccountably interpreted to mean that the honours belong exclusively to Addison. But almost in his next sentence Tickell goes on—" As for the distinct Papers, they were never or seldom shewn to each other, by their respective Authors,"—which is hardly in favour of any elaborate programme or associated action. Indeed, apart from a certain rough agreement as to the first two numbers, or " Prefatory Discourses," there seems to have been no such programme, and any assertion to the contrary prompts the suspicion that the *Spectator*, notwithstanding the famous " *nocturna versate manu, versate diurna* " of Johnson, is more talked about than read. In Number 1, which is undeniably by Addison, he sketched lightly and with his own inimitable touch, that taciturn " Looker-on," whose " Sheet-full of Thoughts " was to appear every morning, Sundays excepted. Following this, in Number 2, which is as unmistakably Steele's, was dashed off the little group of " select Friends " who were to make up the *Spectator* Club, headed by the kit-cat of Sir Roger de Coverley. The other five members were a

Templar, a Clergyman, a Soldier (Captain Sentry) a Merchant (Sir Andrew Freeport) and Will Honeycomb, an elderly fine gentleman and Man of Pleasure. A Committee from this body was to sit nightly in order to inspect " all such Papers as may contribute to the Advancement of the Publick Weal." Some of Addison's advocates have attempted to transfer the credit of this second number from Steele to Addison by suggesting that the characters were "touched" by the latter. But even if the style did not exhibit all the indications of that hasty genius which contrived the "Trumpet Club" in the *Tatler*, the paper is disfigured by a piece of negligent bad taste which makes it more than probable that Addison never saw it until it was published. The passage concerning beggars and gipsies in the description of Sir Roger, is one which Steele's rapid pen may conceivably have thrown off in a hurry ; but it is also one to which Addison—assuming him at this stage to have had the slightest mental idea of the character whose last hours he was afterwards to describe with such effective simplicity —could never have given his *imprimatur*. It is an outrage far less excusable than the historical lapse committed by Tickell, when, in No. 410, he allowed the Knight for a moment to mistake a woman of the town for a " Woman of Honour,"—a mistake, after all, no worse than that later, and more memorable misadventure, where an entire family circle were deceived in the identity of my Lady Blarney and Miss Carolina Wilelmina Amelia Skeggs.

The truth would appear to be, that the character of the Worcestershire baronet, so happily developed in the sequel under the pens of the two friends, was, at the outset, rather a lucky accident of invention than the first stage in a preconceived creation ; and many numbers succeeded to Steele's description of the Club before Sir Roger de Coverley was again seriously presented to the reader. He is indeed mentioned incidentally three or four times in subsequent *Spectators*, but it is not until No. 106 that he really begins to assume the importance which has made him a personage in English Literature. In accordance with a hint casually dropped in No. 46, Addison in No. 106 gives an account of the Coverley household with its old-fashioned ways, which include an old chaplain who understands " a little of Back-Gammon,"[1] and reads the sermons of Tillotson and

---

[1] Swift apparently thought this accomplishment a *sine qua non* in a chaplain. " Can the parson of the parish

Barrow from his pulpit instead of his own compositions. Steele came after with another
paper, on the Coverley servants; and Addison
followed that by the masterpiece of Will
Wimble, the poor gentleman and younger
brother, who is almost as well-known in letters
as the Knight himself. In the next of the
series, Steele, with a hand scarcely less skilful
than that of his colleague, describes the family
picture gallery; and certainly nothing in Addison is happier than its closing touch about the
ancestor who " narrowly escaped being killed
in the Civil Wars " by being " sent out of the
Field upon a private Message, the Day before
the Battel of Worcester." Three papers
farther on, Addison depicts a country Sunday;
and Steele responds with an account of Sir
Roger and the " perverse beautiful Widow " of
the introductory sketch. Then we have Sir
Roger hare-hunting; Sir Roger on his way to
the County-Assizes delivering the time-honoured judgment that " much might be said on
both Sides; " and Sir Roger interviewing the
Gipsies. After this, very little is heard of the
Knight until he comes to London, and goes (by
this time always with Addison) to Westminster

play at backgammon? "—he asks Lady Queensberry,
when he is proposing to visit her at Amesbury.

Abbey, to Drury-Lane Playhouse (to see Anne
Oldfield as Andromache in the *Distrest Mother*
of Mr. Phillips), and to the Spring-Garden at
Vauxhall. The last record of him—for we may
neglect the ambiguous tavern-incident referred
to in our previous paragraph—is the admirable
letter, again by Addison, in which Mr. Biscuit,
the butler, describes his master's last illness and
death. It has been sometimes asserted that
Addison, after the fashion of Cervantes, killed
his hero to prevent greater liberties being taken
with him; but the interval between the Tickell
escapade and the butler's despatch is too wide
to establish any definite connection between the
respective occurrences, and, moreover, the
Club itself was obviously being wound up. Of
its remaining members the authors never made
any material use. In the allotment of the characters, it is but reasonable to suppose that
Addison (in addition to Sir Roger) would have
devoted himself to the Templar and Will
Honeycomb, while the Soldier, the Merchant,
and the Clergyman would fall to the share of
Steele. In practice, however, nothing so definite ever came to pass. After Steele's first
sketch in No. 2, the Clergyman only once re-
appears, while the Templar is little but a name.
Sir Andrew Freeport delivers himself occasion-

ally upon matters of trade, and Captain Sentry occupies a couple of papers. As for the gallant Will Honeycomb, though he can scarcely be styled a *personnage muet*, his chief contribution to the interest of the fable is the marriage to a country girl (in a grogram gown) with which he quits both the Town and the scene. Whether these portraits had actual originals is doubtful. Tickell, who should have been well informed, regarded the whole of the characters as " feigned," and Steele, in No. 262, expressly disclaims the delineation of his contemporaries. The reader, he says, would think the better of him, if he knew the pains he was at in qualifying what he wrote after such a manner, that nothing might be interpreted as aimed at private persons. But his disclaimer has been as futile as the disclaimers of Hogarth and Fielding; and, as usual, Sir Roger and Will Wimble, Captain Sentry and the Widow, have not been allowed to lack for models.

The Coverley sequence and the proceedings of the Club must not, however, be supposed to constitute the sole theme of the *Spectator*, or even to present its chief feature of interest. Something more than the fitful apparition of a few figures whose sayings and doings scarcely occupy fifty papers out of five hundred and

fifty-five must clearly have been required to al-
lure and retain the interest of subscribers whose
enthusiasm survived an increased price and a
prohibitive Stamp Tax.   At this time of day, it
is probable that the graver and more critical
efforts of Addison, and the edifying lay-sermon
which represents the " Christian Hero " side in
Steele would not find a very attentive audience.
But it must be remembered that, when they were
first penned, it was a new thing to discover poetry
in *Chevy Chase* and the *Children in the Wood*,
or to include, in pages professedly occupied
by social sketches and sub-humorous satire, dis-
quisitions upon Death, Benevolence, Ambition,
and Solitude.   Under Anna Augusta, Steele's
moral essays and Addison's criticisms enjoyed
and deserved a vogue which new methods of
analysis and other fashions of exhortation have
long made impossible ; and in the old *Beauties*,
these papers occupy a far larger place than the
studies of contemporary manners and the
sketches of individual types which to us now
form the main attraction of the *Spectator*.   Of
these sketches and studies there are enough and
to spare.   Neither Addison nor Steele, it is true,
ever excelled the " first sprightly runnings " of
the *Tatler*, and it may be doubted if either afterwards produced anything that really rivals

Mr. Bickerstaff's " Visit to a Friend " or (in its kind) the perennial " Ned Softly " of the earlier paper. On the other hand the " Meditations in Westminster Abbey," the " Vision of Mirzah," the " Everlasting Club," the admirable " Citizen's " and " Fine Lady's " Journals, and the various papers on Headdresses, Hoods, Patches, Fans and a hundred other themes belong to Addison and the *Spectator*, while Steele, in the same pages, has many essays which reach the level of his excellent " Death of Estcourt," his " Ramble from Richmond to London," his "Stage Coach Journey "and his " Story of Brunetta and Phyllis." Nothing can give a better notion of the sustained fertility of the two friends than the statement that, out of the abovementioned total of five hundred and fifty-five numbers, more than five hundred were written by Steele and the still nameless " Auxiliary," to whom, at the close, he again, over his own signature, pays grateful tribute. " I am indeed much more proud of his long continued Friendship, than I should be of the Fame of being thought the Author of any Writings which he himself is capable of producing. I remember when I finished the *Tender Husband*, I told him there was nothing I so ardently wished, as that we might some time or other publish a Work written by us both, which should bear the name of the *Monument*, in Memory of our Friendship."

But if Addison's assistance as an anonymous contributor to his friend's enterprise had its advantages, it must be confessed that—as far as that friend is concerned—it also had its drawbacks. Although at first the result was to identify Steele with the entire work much more comprehensively than the circumstances warranted (the old *folio* titles of the *Spectator*, in fact, attribute the whole of the papers to him),[1] upon the other hand he occasionally became personally responsible for utterances not his own, which had given grave offence. So that if, in Swift's words, " he flourish'd by imputed Wit," he also suffered by imputed Satire. " Many of the Writings now published as his [Addison's]," he says in his letter to Congreve, " I have been very patiently traduced and calumniated for ; as they were pleasantries and oblique strokes upon certain of the wittiest men of the Age." When, in Tickell's edition of 1721, Addison's contributions to the *Tatler* were definitely identified, and their extent and

[1] One of these, now before us, runs—" A Compleat Sett of the SPECTATORS, By Richard Steele, Esq., London : Printed for *S. Buckley* and *J. Tonson*, and sold by *A. Baldwin*, near the *Oxford Arms* in *Warwick Lane*, MDCCXIII. "

import thoroughly apprehended, people began
—perhaps naturally at first—to transfer a dis-
proportionate amount of the credit to Addison,
and to assign a much lower place to Steele,
who was sometimes spoken of as if he were no
more than a merely colourless mediocrity, to
whose good fortune it had fallen to farm a
genius.   This reaction, in spite of the protests
of such critics as Lamb, Hazlitt, and Leigh
Hunt, may be said to have culminated in Ma-
caulay's brilliant *Edinburgh* article of 1843 on
Miss Aikin's " Addison."   Here Steele is sys-
tematically depressed to exalt his friend, whose
worst essay—in the great critical special pleader-
er's opinion—was as good as the best essay of
any of his coadjutors.   Twelve years after, in
March, 1855, Mr. John Forster valiantly took
up the cudgels for Steele in the *Quarterly*, and
from this date Steele's character may be said to
have been gradually rehabilitated.   That Addison was the major contributor to the *Spectator*,
and that he had gifts of style and expression to
which his colleague could not pretend, may be
granted.   But it must also be granted that, as
compared with that colleague, he had some very
manifest advantages.   He was, and remained, a
contributor only, working at his ease ; and, in
any failure of fancy, he could—as Tickell allows

—fall back upon long-accumulated material (such as his essays on Milton, Wit, Imagination and the like) to serve his turn. Steele, on the contrary, was not only responsible editor,[1] but sub-editor as well, and when matter or invention ran short, he was obliged to " make up" with the communications of his correspondents. In the way of reserve " copy," he had nothing but a few of his own old love-letters to his wife and a quotation or two from the " *Christian Hero.*" These conditions were not favourable to " correctness," if " correctness " had been his aim ; and they should be taken into account in assessing the relative merits of the two friends, who, it must be noted, never succeeded as well when they worked apart as they succeeded when they worked together. Although they may not have revised each other's writings, it was the conjunction of their individualities which made the *Spectator* what it remains,—the most readable of the Eighteenth-Century Essayists ; and in this conjunction Steele was the originating, and Addison the elaborating, intellect. The primary invention, the creative idea, came from Steele ;

[1] " When a Man has engaged to keep a Stage-Coach," says he in *Tatler* No. 12, "he is obliged, whether he has Passengers or not, to set out." Fielding has the same thought in the " initial essay " to Book II of *Tom Jones.*

the shaping power, the decorative art from Addison.[1] What Steele with his "veined humanity" and ready sympathy derived from "conversation,"—to use the eighteenth-century term for intercourse with the world—he flung upon his paper then and there without much labour of selection; what Addison perceived in his environment when—to use Steele's phrase—he began "to look about him and like his company," he carried carefully home to carve into some gem of graceful raillery or refined expression. Each writer has, naturally, the defects of his qualities. If Addison delights us by his finish, he repels us by his restraint and absence of fervour; if Steele is careless, he is always frank and genial. Addison's papers are faultless in their art, and in this way achieve an excellence which is beyond the reach of Steele's quicker and more impulsive nature. But for words which the heart finds when the head is seeking; for phrases glowing with the white heat of a generous emotion; for sentences which throb and tingle with manly pity or courageous indignation—we must turn to the essays of Steele.

[1] What follows—to obviate laborious paraphrase—is borrowed almost textually from the writer's life of Steele (1886).

" DEAR MRS. DELANY.

MARY GRANVILLE, later Mrs. Pendarves, and eventually Mrs. Delany, was certainly blessed with length of days. She was born in May, 1700, some twenty-one months before Sorrel stumbled over a mole-hill at Hampton Court, and broke the collar-bone of King William the Deliverer. She died in April, 1788, under the third of the Georges, only a few weeks after the opening of the interminable trial of Warren Hastings.

Many events, many changes, came to pass in those five reigns, and eight and eighty years. It was the period of Marlborough's famous battles in Flanders; it was the period of the two Jacobite risings ; of the Seven Years' War ; of the struggle for American Independence ; of the " No Popery " riots of '80. When Mary Granville was a child, people were reading the *Tatler* and *Spectator* in full-bottomed periwigs and elaborate " heads "; at the date of her death the great *Times* itself was being perused by a generation with frizzed hair and pigtails. In her girlhood, she had devoured the " vast French

romances, neatly gilt " of the *Rape of the Lock;*
as a middle-aged woman, in place of the
Scudérys and Calprenèdes, she was absorbed by
the newer methods of Richardson and Fielding;
and she survived to study a fresh variety of
fiction in the *Evelina* and *Cecilia* of Frances
Burney.   Vanderbank and Charles Jervas were
the fashionable painters of her youth ; she out-
lasted the entire artistic career of Hogarth (who
helped to teach her drawing) ; and when at last
her own end came, Gainsborough and Reynolds
were not far from theirs.

During the earlier half of her lifetime, Pope
reigned paramount in poetry, and Milton was
practically forgotten : during the latter half,
people were beginning to forget Pope, and to
remember Milton.   Cowper, and Blake, and
Burns were writing ; the Romantic revival was
in the air.   And not only was Mrs. Delany co-
existent with notabilities ; but she was personally
acquainted with many of them.   She corre-
sponded with Swift ; she was intimate with
Handel, and Garrick, and Horace Walpole ;
she knew Wesley and Hannah More ; she knew
the erudite Mrs. Montagu and the aristocratic
Mrs. Boscawen.   She was the playmate and
associate   of   Matthew   Prior's   " Kitty,"
Catherine Hyde, Duchess of Queensberry and

Dover; she was the lifelong ally of his
" Peggy," Margaret Cavendish Harley,
Duchess of Portland; she was own cousin to
the beautiful Duchess of Devonshire, and she
was the " Dear Mrs. Delany " of " great
George " himself and his consort Queen
Charlotte. Dr. Johnson and Mrs. Thrale, she
did not know, and apparently did not desire to
know. Yet it is the Doctor who has preserved
what another of her friends, Edmund Burke,
had been heard to affirm in her favour. She was
(declared Burke) " a truly great woman of
fashion," and " not only the woman of fashion
of the present age, but the highest bred woman
in the world, and the woman of fashion of
all ages."

For this comprehensive, and yet imperfect
commendation,— for Mary Delany was something more than a mere *grande dame*,— she had
one indispensable qualification, good birth.
Among her ancestors she numbered that heroic
Sir Richard Grenville of Kingsley's *Westward
Ho* and Tennyson's *Revenge*, and his scarcely
less illustrious grandson, the Royalist Sir Bevil,
who has been sung by Hawker of Morwenstow.
Her paternal uncle was George, Lord Lansdowne, that " Granville, the polite," for whom
(*" non injussa cano "*) Pope rhymed *Windsor*

Forest. As her father was a younger son, and consequently a poor man, she was brought up at Whitehall by an aunt, Lady Stanley, one of Queen Mary's maids of honour, and to be a maid of honour she too was at first destined, Queen Anne herself putting down her name for that distinction. But at seventeen another vocation in life was found for her in a queer *mariage de convenance,* her suitor being an old friend of Lord Lansdowne, Mr. William Pendarves of Roscrow, in Cornwall. In addition to the drawback of being nearly sixty, Mr. Pendarves had several eighteenth-century characteristics which were scarcely recommendations. He was as fat as Parson Trulliber; as red faced as Addison's Tory Fox-hunter; as gouty as Lord Chalkstone; and, after wedlock, seems to have contracted or developed the objectionable custom of coming drunk to bed which was observed by Farquhar's Squire Sullen, whom, indeed, he very generally resembled. But "Granville the polite," favoured his advances, going as far even as to threaten to have a rival suitor dragged through the horse-pond; and, in 1717, much against her will, Mary Granville was united to her "Gromio," as she calls him. He, in due time, transferred his bride to a ruinous and Radcliffian castle in Cornwall.

Apart from the detail that he was "furiously jealous," and, as already stated, habitually intemperate, he does not seem to have treated his wife harshly. But when in 1724, he died suddenly, she can scarcely have honestly regretted him, since, against all precedent in such cases, he left her poor.

She had been born with the century, and was consequently still young at her first husband's death. Already, during his lifetime, she had not wanted for admirers, nor did she lack them in her early widowhood. One of her suitors was Lord Baltimore; another Lord Tyrconnel. In 1730, she and her sister Anne, under the style of Aspasia and Selina, carried on a religious flirtation with John Wesley, who had not yet started for Georgia, or experienced the fascinations of the storekeeper's niece at Savannah. Some of Wesley's biographers, indeed, are disposed to think that it would not have taken much to have transformed Mrs. Pendarves into Mrs. Wesley. But her matrimonial experiences had not been promising, and for the present she seems to have preferred to a fresh connection the freedom of a modest income and a large circle of friends. She was fond of drawing and painting (she executed a charming large-eyed picture of the Duchess of

Queensberry) ; and she was a genuine lover of good music, including that unpopular Italian opera against which her master Hogarth had pointed his sharpest etching-needle. In 1731 she went with a friend to Ireland where she stayed at St. Stephen's Green with the Bishop of Killala and his wife, and made acquaintance with Swift, and Swift's friend, Dr. Patrick Delany. Swift seems at once to have admitted her to that select circle of intellectual women whom it pleased him to lecture, pet and patronise, and he wrote to her not unfrequently, both during her stay in Ireland, and after her return to England. " He [Swift] calls himself ' *my master*,' and corrects me when I speak bad English, or do not pronounce my words distinctly," she says. Of her spelling he must be held to have approved, since he does not condemn it. Indeed, he admits that since he was young, there had been a great improvement in this respect. " A woman of quality, who had *excellent* good sense, was formerly my correspondent ; but she scrawled and spelt like a Wapping wench, having been brought up in a court before reading was thought of any use to a female, and I know several others of very high quality with the same defect." Like the Duchess of Queensberry, Mrs. Delany seems to have endeavoured to persuade Swift to come to England, and particularly to Bath,—Bath so conveniently contracted in its comforts and amusements as compared with London, where, owing to its " enormous size," you must spend half the day in getting from one place to another. This was in 1736 (when, as she notes, Fielding was playing *Pasquin* to overflowing audiences); and five and thirty years later, we shall find Mr. Matthew Bramble making the same complaint in *Humphry Clinker*. " Pimlico and Knightsbridge," he says, " are almost joined to Chelsea and Kensington ; and if this infatuation continues for half a century, I suppose the whole county of Middlesex will be covered by brick." What would they say now, these good people, to the London of to-day ! Large or small, however, Swift was not to be lured from the Ireland he hated. " I cannot make shifts," he said in 1734, " lie rough, and be undone by starving in scanty lodgings, without horses, servants, and conveniences." Moreover his deafness and giddiness, as well as other serious ailments, were increasing, and before many months were past, his affairs were in the hands of trustees. After the beginning of 1736 no more letters came to Mrs. Pendarves from the correspondent of whom she had been so proud ; and the only

other reference to him that need be noted here
relates to his aspect not long before his death in
1745. His mental state rendered him a pitiable
sight, though his personal appearance—as is
often the case—had improved with the progress
of his malady. From increasing stoutness, the
hard lines had faded from his face, and his long
silver hair and comely countenance made him a
" very venerable figure."

As already stated, one of the acquaintances
Mrs. Pendarves had made in Ireland was Swift's
friend and subsequent biographer, Dr. Patrick
Delany. It was indeed at Dr. Delany's that
she first met Swift, who was a regular attendant
there on the doctor's reception Thursdays, and
she seems to have been early attracted by
Delany's wit, learning and social qualities.
" Dr. Delany is as agreeable a companion as
ever I met with, and one who condescends to
converse with women, and treat them like reasonable creatures," she says. " These [she had
just been speaking of Wesley] are the sort of
men I find myself inclined to like, and wish I
had such a set in England." A short time before she had written :—" Last Sunday I went to
hear Dr. Delany preach, and was extremely
pleased with him. His sermon was on the
duties of wives to husbands, a subject of no

great use to me at present." At this time
Delany was married. But some years later he
lost his wife ; and eighteen months after that
occurrence, in April, 1743, he proposed to Mrs.
Pendarves. He was then fifty-nine, and she
was nearing forty-three. He made his offer in
an exceedingly manly and straightforward manner, and although by her family the matter
seems to have been covertly regarded as rather
a *mésalliance*, she eventually married him in the
following June. Then after a round of visits,
they took up residence in Clarges Street, pending their return to Ireland, and the obtaining of
preferment for " D. D." [Delany]—a task in
which his wife seems to have been very laudably
active.

Equipped with an admiring husband, and as-
sured of a definite establishment, this is, perhaps, the best moment to attempt some description of Mrs. Delany herself. In her picture by
Opie in the National Portrait Gallery, the frame
of which was designed by Horace Walpole, she
appears as a serene and dignified old lady, who,
in her prime, must have possessed remarkable
personal attractions, as indeed the number and
assiduity of her admirers sufficiently testify.
She had an excellent figure, beautiful shining
hair which curled naturally, a fine red and white

complexion which owed nothing to art, and a
very sweet smile.   Of her eyes, her enthusiastic
second husband declared "that he could never
tell the colour," but to the best of his belief,
"they were what Solomon calls dove's eyes,"
and he adds that " she was almost the only
woman he ever saw whose lips were scarlet and
her bloom beyond expression." For her time
she must have been unusually well educated,
besides   being   an   expert   and   indefatigable
needlewoman, and one of her first enterprises
after her second marriage, was to turn *Paradise
Lost* into an oratorio for Handel.   " She read
and wrote two languages correctly and judi-
ciously."   She was "a mistress of her pen in
every art to which a pen could be applied.   She
wrote a fine hand in the most masterly manner,
and she designed with amazing correctness and
skill."   This was written in 1757.   But it was
only after the death of her affectionate panegyr-
ist that she developed her crowning accomplishment, the famous " paper Mosaiks " now
in the Print Room of the British Museum.
These she commenced, she says, in her seventy-
fourth year, and she continued to work at them
to within five years of her death.   Briefly
described, her method consisted in the minute
piecing together of coloured paper cut so as to

produce accurate imitations of flowers and plants.
In this art she attained a proficiency so extraordinary as to deserve not only the admiration
of Walpole and Reynolds, but of botanists such
as Banks and Erasmus Darwin.   Failing in-
spection of the work itself, those who wish for a
further account of Mrs. Delany's achievements
in this way, cannot do better than consult a
charming *rêverie* on the subject contributed to
Temple Bar for December, 1897, by Mrs.
Edmund Gosse.

This, however, is somewhat to anticipate, as
the famous paper flora was the recreation of
Mrs. Delany's widowed old age, and she had a
long period of wedded happiness as the wife of
Swift's amiable biographer. A bishopric she
did not succeed in obtaining for him ; but she
got him made Dean of Down.   Henceforth her
life was spent between Delville (Dr. Delany's
villa near Dublin, rich with its memories of
Swift and Stella), the Deanery at Down, and
annual visits to England where her old aristocratic friends and particularly the Duchesses of
Queensberry and Portland welcomed her
eagerly.   Her ceaseless industry always kept
her pleasantly busy.   Now she is arranging the
Bulstrode miniatures (" such Petitots, such
Olivers, such Coopers ! ") ; now she is painting

a Madonna and Child for the chapel at Down, or making shell-flowers for its ceiling, now knotting (in " sugar plum " work) interminable chair covers and decorations for Delville whose tapestries and mirrors and marble tables and Japan chests afford her all the pleasures of a proprietor. Then there are long evening readings which give an idea of her likes and dislikes. For Sunday there is Berkeley s *Alciphron*, while of week days Carte's *Life of Ormonde* is a good standing dish. Of Chesterfield's *Œconomy of Life* she approves " all but the chapter on Love " (which, be it said in parenthesis, is harmless to insipidity). Her favourite novelist is Richardson ; and his *Clarissa*, till *Grandison* comes out, her favourite novel. Another much discussed work is not unnaturally Orrery's *Life of Swift*, the errors and ineptitudes of which prompted her husband's own subsequent book on the subject. As perhaps might be expected, Fielding finds little favour with the Delville party. " We are reading Mr. Fielding's *Amelia*," writes Mrs. Delany in 1752. " Mrs. Donnellan and I don't like it at all ; D. D. [the Dean] won't listen to it. Our next important reading will be *Betsy Thoughtless* [Mrs. Heywood's] ; I wish Richardson would publish his *good man* and put all these frivolous authors out of coun-

tenance." Frivolous is scarcely the right word
for Fielding ; and one resents the bracketing
with *Amelia* of the very second-rate *Betsy
Thoughtless.* But Mrs. Donnellan was the
favourite correspondent to whom Richardson
abused his rival ; and Mrs. Delany's sister Mrs.
Dewes was another of the circle of admirers
who were honoured with the good printer's
epistles. Imperfect sympathy with Fielding is
therefore to be anticipated, and we know besides, from Fielding himself, that his last novel
was but coldly received by the fashionable
world.[1] Another of the Delville antipathies is
however more difficult to understand. " The
Dean," says his lady in April, 1760, " is indeed
very angry with the author of *Tristram Shandy*,
and those who do not condemn the work as it
deserves ; it *has not* [entered ?] and *will not*
enter this house, especially now your account is
added to a very bad one we had heard before."
Again, " D. D. is not a little offended with Mr.
Sterne, his book is read here as in London, and
diverts more than it offends." Why Dr. Delany,
who had been the intimate friend of Swift in his
last days, should have drawn so hard a line at
Sterne, of whose masterpiece, moreover, only

[1] See the paper in this volume on *The Covent-Garden
Journal.*

two volumes had appeared, is a point which requires elucidation.

On May 6, 1768, Dr. Delany died, in his eighty-fourth year, and was buried at Delville. By this time his widow was sixty-eight. The last years of her married life had not been without cares arising from money difficulties and the failing health of her husband, after whose death, the Duchess of Portland carried her old friend off for a long visit to Bulstrode (in Bucks), and eventually persuaded her to settle among her friends in London. This she did first in Thatched House Court, Little St. James Street; and, from December, 1771, in St. James's Place, where seventeen years later, she died. She was buried in her parish church of St. James's, where still may be read Bishop Hurd's inscription testifying to her "singular ingenuity and politeness" and her "unaffected piety." Hurd was a dry word-picker and precisian; but these particular epithets are not ill-chosen. Among Mrs. Delany's chief attractions must certainly have been her many accomplishments; and it was no doubt owing to her unvarying amiability and well-bred amenity that she was such an universal favourite. One feels that she must have been good to look at and to live with, and that she must have represented in all its soothing per-

fection that leisured and measured old world
mode of address and conversation which has
departed with the advent of telegrams and snap-
shot portraits. It is easy to conceive her as
the " Dear Mrs. Delany" of her environment,
—as the handsome and wonderful old lady
whom every one delighted to fondle and make
much of (including the Royal Family!); who
was so sympathetic and so lovable, and whose
endless fund of anecdotes of Swift and Pope,
coupled with her extraordinary achievements in
needlework and cut paper (at her age too!)
made her almost a curiosity. Nor must it be
forgotten that, besides being cultivated and accomplished when these things were rare, she
seems to have also been what was rarer still,
a woman of unblemished character in a de-
cidedly difficult society, and, in an unobtrusive
way, sincerely religious.

Her life has been said to have more of anecdote—in the Johnsonian sense—than actual
incident. Nevertheless the two series of her
Autobiography and Correspondence, as edited
by the late Lady Llanover, occupy no fewer
than six bulky volumes. Apart from the grad-
ual disclosure of the singularly composed and
sweet-blooded nature to which we have above
referred, they abound in valuable details of the

social life of the eighteenth century. But their
material is by no means of the kind which can
be lightly summarised in a short paper. There
are too many names and too many occurrences
to be scheduled effectively. Here it is a little
picture of Rousseau's ante-chamber at Paris,
"filled with bird-cages," and guarded by Thérèse
Levasseur, vigilant to protect her *bon mari* from
inconvenient visitors ; here a reference to Handel's blindness, or Mrs. Woffington's admirable
acting of Lady Townly, despite her "disagree-
able voice" and "ungainly arms," or Mrs.
Montagu's "Cupidons" room, which must
have been even more remarkable than the
celebrated Peacock Saloon. "How such a
genius at her age, and so circumstanced, could
think of painting the walls of her dressing-room
with bowers of roses and jessamine, entirely
inhabited by little cupids in all their wanton
ways, is astonishing." Another page shall give
you an excellent report of a visit to Garrick at
Hampton, with a drinking of tea in Shakespeare's temple, under Roubillac's statue, and in
close proximity to the famous Stratford chair
designed by Hogarth ; or a description of a
fête champêtre at Lord Stanley's worthy to pair
off with Walpole's *festino* at Strawberry, or with
the notable entertainment given by Miss Pel-

ham at Esher Place to his Grace the Duc de
Nivernais. Not the least interesting of the
records, as may be anticipated, relate to bygone
pastimes and costumes, in which latter the va-
garies of Miss Chudleigh naturally find a mention. In 1772, she was flaunting it in " a sack
trimmed with roses of ribbon, in each a large
diamond, no cap, and diamonds in her hair; a
tucker edged with diamonds, and no more of a
tippet than makes her fair bosom conspicuous
rather than hides it." Elsewhere there is an
account of Lady Coventry's coiffure, " a French
cap that just covered the top of her head, of
blond, that stood in the form of a butterfly,
with its wings not quite extended, frilled sort
of lappets crossing under her chin, and tied
with pink and green ribbon—a headdress that
would have charmed a shepherd!" Some of
the designs described are extraordinary. That
the Duchess of Queensberry's attire should
have successfully simulated a landscape, with
"brown hills," tree-stumps gilded by the sunlight, and other picturesque accessories, is quite
in keeping with what we know of the lady
whom Walpole named " Sa Singularité." We
must, however, invite the reader to guess to
whom the following extract refers :—" Her
petticoat was of black velvet embroidered with

chenille, the pattern a *large stone vase* filled with *ramping* flowers [the italics are Mrs. Delany's] that spread almost over a breadth . . . from the bottom to the top, between each vase of flowers was a pattern of gold shells and foliage, embossed and most heavily rich." "*Je vous le donne en dix ; je vous le donne en cent*," —as Mme. de Sévigné would say. The person who sported this "laboured piece of finery" was Selina Hastings, Countess of Huntingdon, afterwards the respected head of a special Methodist connection.

THE COVENT-GARDEN JOURNAL.

IN the month of December, 1751, when Henry Fielding issued his last novel of *Amelia*, —that *Amelia* which Johnson, despite his dislike to the author, read through without stopping, —he was close upon forty-five. His health was breaking under a complication of disorders, and he had not long to live. For three years he had been in the Commission of the Peace for Middlesex and Westminster, earning—" by composing, instead of inflaming, the quarrels of porters and beggars," and " by refusing to take a shilling from a man who most undoubtedly would not have had another left—" rather more than £300 per annum of " the dirtiest money upon earth," and even of this a considerable portion went to Mr. Brogden, his clerk. He also received, he tells us in the *Journal of a Voyage to Lisbon*, "a yearly pension out of the public service-money," the amount of which is not stated; and he was in addition, as appears from his will, possessed of twenty shares in that multifarious enterprise, puffed obliquely in Book V of *Amelia*, the

Universal Register Office, which was Estate Office, Lost Property Office, Servants' Registry, Curiosity Shop, and several other things beside. He lived at Bow Street, in a house belonging to his patron, John, Duke of Bedford, which house, during its subsequent tenure by his brother and successor, John Fielding, was destroyed by the Gordon rioters; and he had a cottage or country-box on the highroad between Acton and Ealing, to which he occasionally retired; and where, in all probability, his children lived with his mother-in-law, Mrs. Daniel. It was at this date, and in these circumstances, that he projected the fourth of his newspapers, *The Covent-Garden Journal*, concerning which the following notice is inserted at the end of the second volume of *Amelia*, coming immediately after an advertisement of the Universal Register Office:—"All Persons, who intend to take in THE COVENT-GARDEN JOURNAL, which will be certainly published on *Saturday* the 4th of *January* next, Price 3d. are desired to send their Names, and Places of Abode, to the above Office, opposite *Cecil-Street* in the *Strand*. And the said Paper will then be delivered at their Houses."

In conformity with this announcement, the first number of *The Covent-Garden Journal* duly appeared on Saturday, the 4th January, 1752. It was said to be "by Sir Alexander Drawcansir, Knt. Censor of Great Britain," and was "to be continued every Tuesday and Saturday." It was "Printed, and Sold by Mrs. Dodd, at the *Peacock, Temple-Bar;*" and at the Universal Register Office, "where Advertisements and Letters to the Author are taken in." For the form, it was Cowper's "folio of four pages," beginning with an Essay on the *Spectator* pattern, followed by Covent Garden news, "Occasional Pieces of Humour," "Modern History" from the newspapers "*cum notis variorum,*" Foreign Affairs, and miscellaneous advertisements, in which last the Universal Register Office and its doings naturally play a conspicuous part. In his initial paper, Fielding expressly disclaims Politics, as the term is understood by his contemporaries, *i. e.*, Faction; personal Slander and Scurrility; and Dulness, unless—like his predecessor Steele—he is unable to avoid it. His motive for issuing the paper is not explicitly disclosed; but it may be fairly suggested that the advancement of the Register Office, in which he and his brother were concerned, and the placing on record from time to time of the more important cases that came before him at Bow Street in his

magisterial capacity—were not foreign to his
project. That the latter was intended to be a
prominent feature, is plain from his second
number, where, in promising to make the paper
"a much better Journal of Occurrences than
hath been ever yet printed," he says:—" I have
already secured the Play-houses, and other
Places of Resort in this Parish of Covent
Garden, as I have Mr. Justice Fielding's Clerk,
who hath promised me the most material
Examinations before his Master."

When Cowper described the eighteenth
century newspaper as a " folio of four pages "
he added

> " happy work!
> Which not e'en critics criticise."

To *The Covent-Garden Journal* this is singularly inapplicable, since it not only provoked,
but was calculated to provoke, contemporary
comment. The pioneer of its " Occasional
Pieces of Humour " was "*A Journal of the
Present Paper War between the Forces under
Sir Alexander Drawcansir, and the Army of
Grub-Street.*" In his " Introduction " to this,
Sir Alexander contended that the Press was in
the possession of an army of scribblers; and
that the Government of the State of Criticism
was usurped by incompetent persons, whose

ranks had moreover been swelled by irregulars less competent still in the shape of " Beaux, Rakes, Templars, Cits, Lawyers, Mechanics, School-boys, and fine Ladies,"—from which it must be concluded that the Republic of Letters, even now, has made no exceptional progress. To all this " Swarm of Vandals," the new Censor declared war. His idea was not a strikingly novel one, either in its inception or its execution ; and it is only necessary to quote two passages from this source, because of the events that followed them. In his second number for January 7th, describing the operations of his troops, Fielding proceeds—" A little before our March, however, we sent a large Body of Forces, under the Command of General A. Millar [his publisher], to take Possession of the most eminent Printing-Houses. The greater Part of these were garrisoned by Detachments from the Regiment of Grub-Street, who all retired at the Approach of our Forces. A small Body, indeed, under the Command of one Peeragrin Puckle, made a slight Show of Resistance ; but his Hopes were soon found to be in *Vain* [Vane] ; and, at the first Report of the Approach of a younger Brother of General Thomas Jones, his whole Body immediately disappeared, and totally overthrew some of their

own Friends, who were marching to their
Assistance, under the Command of one
Rodorick Random. This Rodorick, in a
former Skirmish with the People called Critics,
had owed some slight Success more to the
Weakness of the Critics, than to any Merit of
his own."

The not very formidable satire of this passage was evidently levelled at Smollett, whose
Peregrine Pickle had been published at the beginning of 1751, with a success to which its
incorporation into its pages of the scandalous
Memoirs of Francis Anne, Viscountess Vane,
—memoirs which Horace Walpole declared
worthy to be bound up with those of his own
sister-in-law and Moll Flanders,—had, as
Fielding's *jeu de mots* implies, largely contributed. Sir Alexander further relates that his
troops, after being rapturously received by the
Critical garrisons at Tom's in Cornhill and
Dick's at Temple Bar, *blockheaded* up the Bedford Coffee House in Covent Garden, the
denizens of which were divided in their welcome, part of them being overawed by a
nondescript Monster with Ass's ears, evidently
intended for the Lion's Head Letter Box on the
Venetian pattern (now at Woburn Abbey),
which, having honourably served at Button's for

Steele's *Guardian*, was then doing fatigue duty
at the Bedford for the " Inspector " of the very
versatile Dr., or Sir John Hill.   As far as it is
possible to comprehend this somewhat obscure
quarrel, Fielding, at an earlier and accidental
meeting, had jocosely, but injudiciously, proposed to Hill, whom he knew too little, that
they should make believe to attack one another
for the public diversion,—a thing which, if it
had not been much done before, has certainly
been done since.   But Hill, a pompous, un-
scrupulous man, " gave him away " forthwith.
The " Inspector " essays were published in
The London Daily Advertiser, and in No. 268,
two days later, he retorted in a strain of out-
raged dignity.   He told the private story from
his own highly virtuous point of view, declared
that the proposed mock-fight would have been
a disingenuous trifling with a trusting public,
patronised Fielding as a paragraphist, and pronounced him as an essayist to be " unmeaning,
inelegant, confused and contradictory."   He
was even base enough to take advantage of Sir
Alexander's failing health.   " I am sorry " (he
said) " to insult the departed Spirit of a living
Author ; but I tremble when I view this Instance of the transitory Nature of what we are
apt to esteem most our own.   I drop a Tear to

the short Period of human Genius, when I see, after so few Years, the Author of *Joseph Andrews* doating in *The Covent-Garden Journal.* I have an unaffected Pain in being made the Instrument of informing him of this: I could have wished him to enjoy for Life that Opinion he entertains of himself; and never to have heard the Determination of the World." Elsewhere he commented ironically on the "particular Orthography" of the word "Blockade," and altogether scored in a fashion which must have been most galling to Fielding, and is to-day almost inconceivable to those who keep in mind the relative importance which posterity has assigned to the performances of "the Author of *Amelia*" (as Hill styled him) and the performances of the Author of the *Adventures of Lady Frail.*[1] Fielding was, no doubt, intensely disgusted, and the next installment of the *Journal of the War*, after giving briefly his own version of the affair, wound up by observing, with more bitterness than usual, that "*his Lowness* [Hill] was not only among the meanest of those who ever drew a Pen, but was absolutely the vilest Fellow that ever wore a Head."[2]

[1] This, which came out in 1751, was a variation by Hill upon the story of Lady Vane.

[2] To prove that Fielding's character of Mr. Inspector

Humiliating, however, as was the procedure of Hill, it was nothing to the action of Smollett a few days subsequently. Seeing that, months before, in the first edition of *Peregrine Pickle*, Smollett had ridiculed Fielding's friend, Lyttelton, as " Gosling Scrag,"—seeing also that he had unprovokedly sneered at Fielding himself for " marrying his own cook-wench " (his second wife, it will be remembered, had been the first Mrs. Fielding's maid), and for settling down " in his old age, as a trading Westminster justice " (in which capacity he certainly never deserved the qualifying adjective), it might be thought that the already-quoted allusions to Smollett in *The Covent-Garden Journal* were neither very virulent nor very vindictive. But such as they were, they stung Smollett to madness. On the 20th of January, he rushed into the fray with a sixpenny pamphlet, modelled after Pope's attack on Dennis, and pur-

was deserved, it is only necessary to read the account of Hill's dealings with Christopher Smart (*Gentleman's Magazine*, 1752, pp. 387, 599). A few months after the above attack on Fielding, he was publicly caned at Ranelagh by Mr. Mounteford Brown, an Irish gentleman whom he had libelled. But he must have been clever, since by impudence, cheap science and scandal, he occasionally contrived to clear £1,500 a year at the pen, in days when Fielding and Goldsmith and Johnson remained poor.

porting to be *A Faithful Narrative of the Base and inhuman Arts That were lately practised upon the Brain of Habbakkuk Hilding, Justice, Dealer, and Chapman, Who now lies at his House in Covent Garden, in a deplorable State of Lunacy, a dreadful Monument of false Friendship and Delusion. By Drawcansir Alexander, Fencing-Master and Philomath.* Little beyond the title-page of this unsavoury performance deserves quotation, for it is indescribably coarse and hopelessly rancorous ; and indeed is only to be explained by its writer's conviction that Fielding's ridicule must be stopped at all hazards, even if it were needful to have recourse to that nauseous, and now obsolete, mode of warfare described by Commodore Trunnion as "heaving in stink-pots."[1] It is also manifest from some of its utterances that Smollett, rightly or wrongly, regarded Fielding's enterprise as inspired by Lyttelton (*cf.* the "false Friendship" of the title) ; and that he was also conceited or foolish enough to believe that Fielding's Partridge and Miss Matthews were borrowed from his own Strap and Miss Wil-

[1] "For the benefit of the curious," Mr. W. E. Henley has reprinted the *Faithful Narrative,* with a prefatory note, at pp. 167–186 of Vol. XII of his complete edition Smollett.

liams. To the Smollett pamphlet, as well as to
some similar and simultaneous attacks upon
himself and *Amelia* in a periodical by Bonnel
Thornton entitled *Have at You All; or, The
Drury Lane Journal,* Fielding made no discernible answer. Already in his fifth issue (January 18th), he had referred generally to " the
unfair Methods made use of by the Enemy ; "
as well as to the impracticability of replying
effectually with a broadsword to blunderbusses
loaded with ragged bullets and discharged
"from lurking Holes and Places of Security."
With the preceding number the *Journal of the
War* had been terminated by the conclusion of
a peace, and a Court of Censorial Enquiry was
announced in its place.

From all this, it must be concluded that, as
Richardson said, Sir Alexander had been
" overmatched by people whom he had de-
spised," and that, when he entered light-heart-
edly upon the campaign against Dulness under
the motto *Nulla venenato est Litera mista Joco,*
he had not anticipated the kind of treatment he
received, or had forgotten that the popular reply
to raillery is abuse. Richardson's words, indeed, are that he had been "overmatched in
his own way." But this is not the case. His
way was possibly the coarse way of his period ;

but it was not the mean and cowardly way of
his assailants.   It is, however, characteristic of
his sensitive nature that the first work he
brought before the new tribunal was his own
Amelia.   He had obviously been greatly an-
noyed by the malicious capital extracted by the
critics out of his unlucky neglect to specify
that Mrs. Booth had been cured of the accident
recorded in the novel (Bk. II., ch. i.).   The
accident was one which had happened to his
first wife, whose charms had apparently been
unimpaired by it ; but he had forgotten to state
in express terms that the Miss Harris of the
story was in similar case ; and had thus given
opportunity to the adversary to mock at his
heroine as " a Beauty without a Nose."
" Amelia, even to her noselessness, is again his
first wife "—wrote Richardson to Mrs. Donnellan ; and Johnson also speaks of that " vile
broken nose, never cured."   In the third number of *The Covent-Garden Journal* (and immediately preceding an announcement of the
thirteenth elopement from her Lord of Lady
Vane), Fielding consequently issued a paragraph upon the subject :—" It is currently reported that a famous Surgeon, who absolutely
cured one Mrs. Amelia Booth, of a violent
Hurt in her Nose, insomuch, that she had

scarce a Scar left on it, intends to bring Actions against several ill-meaning and slanderous People, who have reported that the said Lady had no Nose, merely because the Author of her History, in a Hurry, forgot to inform his Readers of that Particular . . ." Besides this, he made several additions to the book itself which left no doubt upon the subject. But he was also mortified and depressed by the reception which *Amelia* had received from some of those critical irregulars whose activity he had deprecated in his third number, especially the Beaux and fine Ladies, who—if we may believe Mrs. Elizabeth Carter—were unanimous in pronouncing the story "to be very sad stuff."[1] Accordingly, in Number 7, *Amelia* is brought to the Bar, as indicted upon the Statute of Dulness; and Mr. Counsellor Town enumerates her Errors. The book is affirmed to be "very sad Stuff" (thus corroborating Mrs. Carter), and the heroine is described as "a low Character," a "Milksop" and "a Fool." She is reproached with lack of spirit and too frequent fainting; with "servile offices," such as dressing her children and cooking; with being too forgiving to her husband; and lastly with the results of the mishap already sufficiently re-

[1] *Letters,* 3d Ed. 1819, i. 368.

ferred to.   Dr. Harrison and Colonel Bath
fare no better; and finally Mr. Town under-
takes to prove that the Book " contains no Wit,
Humour, Knowledge of human Nature, or of
the World; indeed, that the Fable, moral
Characters, Manners, Sentiments, and Diction,
are all alike bad and contemptible." After
some hearsay evidence has been tendered, and
a " Great Number of Beaus, Rakes, fine
Ladies, and several formal Persons with bushy
Wigs, and Canes at their Noses," are preparing
to supplement it, a grave Man stands up, and
begging to be heard, delivers what must be regarded as Fielding's final apology for his last
novel.

" If you, Mr. Censor, are yourself a Parent,
you will view me with Compassion when I declare I am the Father of this poor Girl the
Prisoner at the Bar; nay, when I go farther,
and avow, that of all my Offspring she is my
favourite Child.   I can truly say that I be-
stowed a more than ordinary Pains in her Education; in which I will venture to affirm, I followed the Rules of all those who are acknowl-
edged to have writ best on the Subject; and if
her Conduct be fairly examined, she will be
found to deviate very little from the strictest
Observation of all those Rules; neither Homer

nor Virgil pursued them with greater Care than myself, and the candid and learned Reader will see that the latter was the noble model, which I made use of on this Occasion.

"I do not think my Child is entirely free from Faults. I know nothing human that is so ; but surely she does not deserve the Rancour with which she hath been treated by the Public. However, it is not my Intention, at present, to make any Defence ; but shall submit to a Compromise, which hath been always allowed in this Court in all Prosecutions for Dulness. I do, therefore, solemnly declare to you, Mr. Censor, that I will trouble the World no more with any Children of mine by the same Muse."

This was recorded by the Censor to the satisfaction of the majority. "Amelia was delivered to her Parent, and a Scene of great Tenderness passed between them, which gave much Satisfaction to many present." But there were some, we are told, who regretted this finish to the cause, and held that the lady ought to have been honourably acquitted. Richardson was not one of these, and wrote jubilantly to Mrs. Donnellan : "Mr. Fielding has overwritten himself, or rather *under*-written ; and in his own journal [which R. persists in calling the

Common Garden Journal] seems ashamed of his last piece ; and has promised that the same Muse shall write no more for him.   The piece, in short, is as dead as if it had been published forty years ago, as to sale."   Then comes the remarkable—" You guess that I have not read *Amelia.*   Indeed, I have read but the first volume."   It was not Amelia, however, of whom Fielding was ashamed ; it was the pub-lic.   Faults of haste and taste he might have committed ; but at least he had presented them with what Thackeray has called " the most de-lightful portrait of a woman that surely ever was painted," and they had preferred the *Adven-tures of Lady Frail.*

The " Court of Censorial Enquiry " con-tinued to sit after this ; but, as the paper pro-gressed, only at rare intervals.   One of its next duties was to cite the new actor Mossop for daring to act Macbeth while Garrick was alive,—a case which was decided, and rightly decided, in favour of Mossop.   Another topic dealt with by the Court was the advertisement in the guise of a criminal of a whole-length print of the notorious Miss Mary or Molly Blandy (shortly afterwards executed at Oxford), before she had been tried, a course which the Court declared to be " base and infamous " as tending to " prepossess the Minds of Men," and " take away that Indifference with which Jurymen ought to come to the Trial of a Prisoner "—a view which it is difficult to gainsay. One of the first books to be examined is the philological *Hermes* of James Harris, a second issue of which had appeared in 1751. But Harris, like the first Mrs. Fielding, was " of Salisbury," and was probably known to " Mr. Censor," who certainly uses him more gently than Johnson, who found bad grammar in his Dedication and coxcombry in himself as an author.[1] A second work, James Gibbs's translation of Bishop Osòrio's *History of the Portuguese*, probably owed the notice it received to its dedication to Lyttelton. But Fielding seems to have refrained from any record of another book inscribed to himself, and frequently advertised in the *Journal*, namely, the third edition of Francis Coventry's *Pompey the Little*, concerning which the quidnuncs

[1] To quote but one statement from Johnson, is seldom safe. Tyers says that the posthumous volumes of Mr. Harris of Salisbury had attractions that engaged the great man to the end. It was *Hermes*, by the way, which Joseph Cradock's friend took for a novel; and when he returned it, mildly deprecated " these imitations of *Tristram Shandy*."

asserted that its Lady Tempest had her proto-
type in Ethelreda Harrison, Viscountess Town-
shend, who was also suspected by some to have
sat for the Lady Bellaston of *Tom Jones.* The
new issue of Sarah Fielding's *David Simple,*
another frequent appearance, was less in need
of the Censor's notice, since the volumes
already included prefaces, avowed and un-
avowed, from his pen. To his friend Hogarth's
Analysis of Beauty, which was announced in
March as a forthcoming Tract in Quarto, he
might perhaps have been expected to give a
hearty welcome; but by the time that much-
edited masterpiece was published in December,
The Covent-Garden Journal itself was no more.
The only literary work belonging strictly to
1752 which it reviewed, was *The Female
Quixote; or, The Adventures of Arabella,* by
Mrs. Charlotte Lenox, whom Fielding, in his
later *Voyage to Lisbon,* describes vaguely as
"shamefully distress'd." To posterity, however, she must always seem rather fortunate
than otherwise; since a lady whose abilities,
or personal charms, were able to procure for
her the countenance and assistance of nearly
all the foremost literary men of her time, cannot justly be counted evil-starred. Johnson
wrote her Prefaces; Goldsmith, her Epilogues;

Garrick helped her to plays (and produced them at Drury Lane); Richardson read her his private letters; and lastly Fielding, in *The Covent-Garden Journal* for March the 24th, after implying that, in some particulars, she had outdone Cervantes himself, declared her *Arabella* to be "a most extraordinary and most excellent Performance." "It is indeed," he went on, "a Work of true Humour, and cannot fail of giving a rational, as well as very pleasing, Amusement to a sensible Reader, who will at once be instructed and very highly diverted." Sir Alexander was never slow at "backing of his friends." Only a week or two before, he had added to a notification in the *Journal* of Mrs. Clive's benefit, the following—"Mrs. Clive in her Walk on the Stage is the greatest Actress the World ever saw; and if as many really understood true Humour as pretend to understand it, she would have nothing to wish, but that the House was six Times as large as it is." It is pleasant to think that he could still write thus of the accomplished comedian, of whom, eighteen years before, he had said in the epistle prefixed to *The Intriguing Chambermaid*, that her part in real life was that of "the best Wife, the best Daughter, the best Sister, and the best Friend."

The laurels of Fielding were not won as a periodical writer; and it is idle to seek in *The Covent-Garden Journal* of his decline for qualities which were absent from *The Champion* and *The True Patriot*. Hill's verdict on his work as an essayist is, of course, simply impertinent; but one of his best critics has also admitted of these particular papers that " few are marked by talent and not one by genius." It is possible, indeed, that they are not all from his pen, as they frequently bear different initials ; and it may well be that some of them should have been signed Lyttelton or Murphy. Many, however, may be certainly attributed to Fielding, *e. g.*, the one containing the " Modern Glossary," which defines the word " Great " to signify Bigness, when applied to a Thing, and often Littleness, or Meanness, when applied to a Man,—a distinction which has the very ring of *Jonathan Wild ;* and the two papers devoted to ridiculing the proceedings of the Robin Hood Society in Essex Street, to which institution he subsequently referred in the *Voyage to Lisbon*. This freethinking club was nevertheless a nursery of rhetoric, in which even Burke is supposed to have exercised his powers ; and its president, a very dignified baker (whom Derrick said ought to have been Master of the

Rolls), was undoubtedly a born orator to boot. One of the subsequent papers tells the story of Jucundo from Ariosto's *Orlando* in the prose fashion afterwards employed by Leigh Hunt in *The Indicator;* and there are lucubrations upon People of Fashion, Humour, Contempt, Profanity and so forth, besides a very sensible and pleasant Dialogue at Tunbridge Wells, "after the Manner of Plato," between a Fine Lady and a Philosopher, which, however, bears the initial "J." But Fielding is clearly responsible for the succeeding number, a skit upon the perverse ingenuities of Shakespearean emendation.

To the student, *The Covent-Garden Journal* must always be interesting for its references, direct and indirect, to its responsible author, now a broken, over-burdened man, nearing the close of his career. Some of these references, hitherto only reported imperfectly from *The Gentleman's Magazine* and elsewhere, have already been dealt with at the outset of this paper. A few others may find a place here. Foremost comes the constantly recurring notification, which shows how little he regarded his office from the point of view of his own Justice Thrasher :—

"All Persons who shall for the Future suffer by Robbers, Burglars, etc., are desired immediately to bring, or send, the best Description they can of such Robbers, etc., with the Time and Place, and Circumstances of the Fact, to Henry Fielding, Esq., at his House in Bow-Street."

Another instance of his energy in his calling is supplied by the collection of cases which, under the title of *Examples of the Interposition of Providence, in the Detection and Punishment of Murder*, he threw into pamphlet form in April, 1752, and which was prompted, as the Advertisement puts it, "by the many horrid Murders committed within this last Year." Copies of the *Examples* were freely distributed in Court to those to whom they seemed likely to be of use. A notice of the arrival at the Register Office of a consignment of Glastonbury Water is proof that Fielding retained his faith in the healing virtues of that "salubrious Spring"; while the announcement of a new translation of *Lucian* in collaboration with William Young ("Parson Adams") testifies to the fact that he still hankered after his old literary pursuits. To this last never-executed project the *Journal* devoted a leading article, which is interesting from its incidental admission that Lucian had been Fielding's own master in style. It further declared that the then-existing English versions of the Samosatene gave no better idea of his spirit "than the vilest Imitation by a Sign-post Painter can convey the Spirit of the excellent Hogarth,"—another instance of Fielding's fidelity to the friend he had praised in the Preface to *Joseph Andrews*. The article ends by trusting the Public will support two gentlemen, "who have hitherto in their several Capacities endeavoured to be serviceable to them, without deriving any great Emolument to themselves from their Labours." In the next number (for July 4th) there is a hint of Sir Alexander's retirement, which was compromised by changing the *Journal* from a bi-weekly to a weekly organ. In that form it continued to appear until November 25th, when Fielding definitely took leave of his readers in the tone of a sad and weary man. He begged the Public that henceforth they would not father upon him the dulness and scurrility of his worthy contemporaries, "since I solemnly declare that unless in revising my former Works, I have at present no Intention to hold any further Correspondence with the gayer Muses." Such engagements are not unfrequently made in moments of illhealth or depression; but in this case the promise was kept. The world would be poorer without the posthumous tract which tells the touching story of Fielding's *Voyage to Lisbon*, and, practically, of his remaining years ; but, unapproached as is that record for patient serenity and cheerful courage, the gayer Muses cannot justly be said to have had anything to do with its production.

Only a limited selection of the essays in *The Covent-Garden Journal* is included in Andrew Millar's edition of Fielding's works. Sets of the original numbers, including the advertisements, etc., are exceedingly rare, and generally incomplete. By way of postscript to this paper we cull a few dispersed items from the chronicle entitled " Modern History." Robberies on the highway are of course as " plenty as blackberries"; but the following extract suggests a picture by Mr. Waller or Mr. Dendy Sadler :—

" A few Days since [this was in January, 1752]. as two Gentlemen of the Army, and two Ladies, were coming from Bath to London, in a returned Coach, they were stopped at the Entrance of a Lane by a Labourer from out of a Field, who told them there were two Highwaymen in the Lane, whose Persons and Horses he described : Upon which the Gentlemen got out of the Coach, and walked, one on each Side of it, with Pistols in their Hands. One of the Ladies, seeing the Gentlemen's Swords in the Coach, said she would not stay in it, but took one and walked by the Side of the Gentlemen ; and, encouraged by her Example, the other Lady did so, by the other Gentleman. Thus armed, they went down the Lane, where they met the Highwaymen, who passed them without the least Molestation."

These incidents, however, were not always picturesque :—

"Wednesday Night [January 15th],. Mr. George Cary, a Higgler, who lived near Epping, on his Return home from Leadenhall-market, was robbed and murdered by three Footpads near the Windmill, which is within half a Mile of his own House : They likewise shot his Son, who was in the Cart with him, but his Wound is not likely to prove mortal. Mr. Cary was an honest, industrious Man, and has left a Wife and five Children."

In his *Enquiry into the Causes of the late Increase of Robbers*, Fielding had advocated private executions in preference to the degrading " Tyburn holidays " of his age. He often returns to the subject in *The Covent-Garden*

Journal, witness the following under date of
April 27th :—

"This Day five Malefactors were executed
at Tyburn. No Heroes within the Memory of
Man ever met their Fate with more Boldness
and Intrepidity, and consequently with more
felonious Glory."

Again,—

"On Monday last [July 13th] eleven
Wretches were executed at Tyburn, and the
very next Night one of the most impudent
Street-Robberies was committed near St.
James's Square ; an Instance of the little Force
which such Examples have on the Minds of the
Populace."

Elsewhere he says (March 27th), concluding
an account which might well be a comment on
the last plate but one of Hogarth's *Apprentice*
series :—

"The real Fact at present is, that instead of
making the Gallows an Object of Terror, our
Executions contribute to make it an Object of
Contempt in the Eye of a Malefactor ; and we
sacrifice the Lives of Men, not for [the italics
are Fielding's] *the Reformation, but the
Diversion of the Populace.*"

Here is a note to Mr. Hartshorne's *Hanging
in Chains :—*

" On Saturday Morning [June 6th] early the Gibbet on Stamford-Hill Common, on which Hurlock hung in Chains for the Murder of his Bedfellow, a few Years since in the Minories, was cut down, and the Remains of Hurlock carried off."

The next is a smuggling episode :—

" [*Monday*, September 11th] Last Week a Riding Officer, with the Assistance of some Dragoons, seized upwards of 300 Weight of Tea and some Brandy (which were lodged in an old House) near Goodhurst in Sussex, and conveyed it to the Custom-house."

In Fielding's century John Broughton (beloved of Borrow !), Jack Slack and Tom Faulkener, were familiar pugilistic names. At this time, Broughton, " the unconquered," had been badly beaten by Slack, and his patron, the Duke of Cumberland, who had made him a Yeoman of the Guard, was said to have lost some £10,000 by his defeat.

" Yesterday [May 13th] at Broughton's Amphitheatre [in Hanway Street, Oxford Street], the Odds on mounting the Stage were two to one against Falkener. About the Middle of the Battle the Odds run against Slack. But the brave Butcher [Slack], after a severe Contest of 27 Minutes and a Half, left his Antagonist prostrate on the Stage, deprived of Sight and in a most miserable Condition. As the House was crouded and Prices were very high, it is computed that there was not less taken than 300*l.*"

The unhappy woman referred to in the ensuing quotation has already been mentioned in the course of this paper. It is only fair to add that she died denying the crime with which she was charged :—

" On Tuesday Morning [March 3d] about 8 o'Clock, Miss Mary Blandy was put to the Bar at the Assizes at Oxford, Mr. Baron Legge and Mr. Baron Smythe being both on the Bench, and tried on an Indictment for poisoning her late Father, Mr. Francis Blandy, Town Clerk of Henly upon Thames ; and after a Trial, which lasted till half an Hour after Eight in the Evening, she was found guilty on very full Evidence, and received Sentence to be hanged."

She was executed on the Castle green at Oxford on Monday, April 6th, in the presence of about 5,000 spectators, " many of whom, and particularly several gentlemen of the university, shed tears," says Sylvanus Urban. Gibbon, who had just come to Oxford, may have witnessed this occurrence.

" Yesterday [November 9th] a Boy climbed up to the Top of the Door of Westminster-hall, in order to see the Lord-Mayor pass by, and missing his hold fell down, and was so much wounded by the Fall and trod under Foot, before he was got out of the Crowd, that it is thought he cannot live."

The Lord Mayor in this instance was the Crispe Gascoyne who, in the following year, took part against Fielding over the case of Elizabeth Canning. Here is a reference to another " person of importance in his Day " :—

" *Bath, Aug.* 24*th* . . . Last Monday a very curious Statue, in white Marble, of Richard Nash, Esq.; done by Mr. Prince Hoare, was erected in the Pump-Room of this City. The Expence is defray'd by several of the principal Inhabitants of this Place, out of Gratitude for his well-known prudent Management for above forty Years, with Regard to the Regulations of the Diversions, the Accommodation of Persons resorting hither, and the general Good of the City."

Was it not Balzac who wrote *Où mènent les Mauvais Chemins?* Here, finally, is the epitaph of that " Charming Betty Careless " whose name figures both in *Amelia* and in the terrible Bedlam scene of *The Rake's Progress* :—

" On Wednesday Evening [April 22d] last was buried from the Parish-House of Covent-Garden, Mrs. Careless, well known for many Years by the Name of *Betty Careless*, by the gay Gentlemen of the Town, of whose Money she had been the Occasion (as it is said) of spending upward of fifty thousand Pounds, tho' at last reduced to receive Alms from the Parish. Almost a certain Consequence attending Ladies in her unhappy Cast of Life."

ON CERTAIN QUOTATIONS IN WAL-
TON'S "ANGLER."

THE *Compleat Angler*, says that accomplished fisherman and poet, the late Thomas Westwood,[1] "is essentially a book to be loved, and to be discoursed of lovingly." Speech censorious or pedantic of Izaak Walton would be as ungrateful as to speak pedantically or censoriously of that other revered author, Charles Lamb, under whose roof Mr. Westwood, as a small boy, first made acquaintance with what he terms "England's one perfect Pastoral." It was a battered copy of Hawkin's issue of 1760, picked up among the rubbish of a marine store, and concerning which, shaded by an ancient apple-tree in the "little overgrown orchard" at Enfield, St. Charles would

[1] It seems but yesterday (1888) that Thomas Westwood died, and (since he has no niche in the *Dictionary of National Biography*) entered into "the portion of weeds and outworn faces." But the author of *The Quest of the Sancgreall* deserves to be remembered (with Hawker of Morwenstow) by all good Arthurians, as the author of *The Chronicle of the "Compleat Angler"* deserves to be remembered by all good fishermen.

157

hold forth to his young friend. Though no fisherman, Lamb, as we know, loved his *Angler.* " It would sweeten a man's temper at any time to read it," he wrote to Coleridge ; and Westwood tells us that the Enfield sitting-room was decorated by copies of Wale's designs to the book, which Emma Isola (Procter's " Isola Bella whom the poets love ") had executed for the delectation of her adopted father.   Where are those precious relics now, and what would they fetch at Christie's !

But though it is pleasant to connect Lamb and Walton, our present concern is with Walton alone, and more especially with the unconventional method of quotation which he frequently adopts.   An immediate example will be better than an exordium.   In his opening chapter, he professes to reproduce a passage from Montaigne ; and in his first edition of 1653, he gives its source in the margin of the page :— " The Lord Montagne in his Apol [ogie] for Ra [ymond] Sebond."   Here is the passage, as he finally revised and readjusted it at pp. 5, 6 of his fifth impression of 1676.   " When my Cat and I entertain each other with mutual apish tricks (*as playing with a garter*) who knows but that I make my Cat more sport than she makes me ? shall I conclude her to be simple, that has

her time to begin or refuse to play as freely as
I myself have ? Nay, who knowes but that it
is a defect of my not understanding her language (for doubtless Cats talk and reason with
one another) that we agree no better : and who
knows' but that she pitties me for being no wiser,
than to play with her, and laughs and censures
my follie, for making sport for her, when we
too play together ? " " Thus freely speaks
Mountaigne concerning Cats,"—says honest
Izaak, concluding his quotation ; but the freedom is not Montaigne's. For when we com-
pare the original French (Didot's ed. 1859, p.
226), what we find is this :—" Quand ie me joue
à ma chatte, qui sçait si elle passe son temps de
moy, plus que ie ne fois d'elle ? nous nous en-
tretenons de singeries reciproques : si i'ay mon
heure de commencer on de refuser, aussi a elle
la sienne." In Florio's version of 1603, this is
thus rendered, " When I am playing with my
Cat, who knowes whether she have more sport
in dallying with me, than I have in gaming with
her ? We entertaine one another with mutuall
apish trickes. If I have my houre to begin or
to refuse, so hath she hers." Now where did
Walton get his version? Obviously he had
seen Florio, witness the " entertain each other
with mutual apish tricks." But there is no

garter, either in the original or in " Resolute John." Unless, therefore, we are to suppose that Walton, like Lord St. Alban, garbled his quotations, we are reduced to the conclusion that he must have written from memory and expanded unconsciously. Yet he prints the passage in inverted commas, as if it were textual.[1]

Bacon not only garbled his quotations ; but he, too, misrepresented Montaigne. " Mountaigny saith prettily," he writes in his Essay "Of Truth," whereas Montaigne expressly tells us that he is quoting " *un ancien,*"—as a matter of fact, Plutarch. Bacon's biographer, Dr. Rawley, extenuates the garbling, like the loyal biographer he was. " If he [Bacon] had occasion to repeat another man's words after him, he had an use and faculty to dress them in better vestments and apparel than they had before : so that the author should find his own speech much amended and yet the substance of it still retained." This may perhaps be the de-

---

[1] This passage in Montaigne seems also to have found its way into the vast drag-net of Butler :

" For 't has been held by many, that
As *Montaigne* playing with his Cat,
Complains she thought him but an Ass,
Much more she would Sir *Hudibras,*" etc.
Hudibras, Part I, canto i, ll 37–40.

fence of our next citation from the *Compleat
Angler*. At the end of an Address "to the
Honest and Judicious Reader" in Francis
Hickes's *Select Dialogues of Lucian*, Oxford,
1634, 4to, is an epigram in Greek and English
signed "T. H.," *i. e.*, Thomas Hickes, the
translator's son and publisher. The English
runs as follows, and is headed, " LUCIAN upon
his booke : "

> *Lucian* well skill'd in old toyes this has writ :
> For all's but folly that men thinke is wit :
> No settled judgement doth in men appeare ;
> But thou admirest that which others jeere.

In Walton's first chapter, just after the Montaigne passage in the first edition, but preceding
it in the fifth, he prints an epigram which he
says is to be found " fix'd before the Dialogues
of *Lucian*." " I have taken a little pleasant
pains [he continues] to make such a conversion
of it as may make it the fitter for all of that
Fraternity "[1] (*i. e.*, of Scoffers):

> *Lucian* well skill'd in *scoffing*, this hath writ
> Friend, that's your folly which you think your wit :
> This you vent oft, void both of *wit* and *fear*,
> Meaning another, when yourself you jeer.

[1] This admission is omitted in the fifth edition of 1676.

That is to say, he has given it an entirely different turn.   It may well be, however, that Walton's views of the sanctity of his text were less
stringent than ours.   A few pages further on
he quotes from Herbert's *Temple*.   Out of the
long poem entitled *Providence* he takes verses
36, 8 and 7, and prints them in that order to
make a "sweet conclusion" to his discourse,
altering a word at the beginning for the sake of
symmetry.   This is not much, for, in another
place, in Chapter XVI, where he cannot remember, he improvises.   In Piscator's song,
"Oh the gallant Fisher's life," which, in the
fifth edition, is attributed to Chalkhill, he makes
the singer say that, " having forgotten a part of
it, I was forced to patch it up by the help of my
own Invention, who am not excellent at Poetrie,
as my part of the song may testifie."   He was
more excellent than he knew, witness his
"composure" in Chapter V of *The Angler's
Wish*, with its pretty reference to his second
wife and his dog Bryan.

Let us turn now to Walton's treatment of
Bacon, to whose *Natural History* and *History
of Life and Death* he makes several references.
He says twice that Sir Francis Bacon (as he
uniformly calls him) puts the age of a Salmon at
not above ten years.   Bacon, in his *History of*

Life and Death (Rawley's version), 1650, p. 11, s. 46, certainly says this of the " *Carp, Breame, Tench, Eele,* and the like," but not of the Salmon. In his other references to the *History of Life and Death,* however, Walton is practically accurate. But in a passage professing to come from the *Naturall History,* it is again necessary to cross-question his quotation. Speaking of water in Chapter V he says that "Sir Francis Bacon, in the Eighth Century of his *Naturalt History,*" "there proves that waters may be the medium of sounds by demonstrating it thus : ' That if you knock two stones together very deep under the water, those that stand on a bank near to that place may hear the noise without any diminution of it by the water.' He also offers the like experiment concerning the letting an anchor fall, by a very long cable or rope, on a rock, or the sand, within the sea." The raw material of this is undoubtedly to be found in Bacon's Eighth Century, Ex. 792 (which Walton gives in the margin) ; but to represent the statement so specifically cited, there is nothing save—" If you dash a *Stone* against a *Stone* in the Bottome of the Water, it maketh a *Sound.*" Perhaps this informality of repetition is part of that unbraced " picture of his disposition,"—to which he refers in his Address to the

Reader,—" in such days and times as I have laid aside business, and gone a-fishing."

There is, of course, another, and a not unreasonable solution of these things, namely, that Walton may have obtained his information by word of mouth from friends who did not, and perhaps did not pretend to speak with absolute accuracy. In his first chapter he says distinctly that Piscator's "philosophical discourse" is most of it derived from a recent conference with his friend, the famous anatomist and Gresham professor, Dr. Thomas Warton ; and in a subsequent chapter (the nineteenth) where he gives an account of a " strange fish," he introduces what he has to tell by admitting that he has " been beholding " to his learned friend " for many of the choicest observations that he has imparted " to his scholar. It is to be observed, too, in this instance, that though he apparently received his data orally, he prints the passage in italics, like a textual quotation. This system of instruction by conference would explain many things which otherwise are difficult to understand, as, for example, the reference in Chapter I to the *Voyages* of Mendez Pinto, with their mention of " a king and several priests a-fishing." Those who take the trouble to look up Chapter LXXIX of Henry

Cogan's folio version of 1653, to which Walton's
editors direct him, will discover with surprise
that the only discernible passage on the subject
is a detailed account of the baiting by the King of
Bungo of a huge *Whale* which he has " cooped
up in a channel," and that of clerical Brothers
of the Angle there is never a word. It is clear
that Walton could not have seen his authority
if Major's reference be correct. When he has
seen his authority, he is usually precise enough.
For example, he had evidently consulted the
Travels of George Sandys, the translator of
Ovid, for though he professes to quote from
memory, he quotes accurately. He was also
experimentally familiar with that curious old
book, Dr. George Hakewill's *Apologie or
Declaration of the Power and Providence of God
in the Government of the World*, Printed for
Robert Allott, at the Beare in Paules Churchyard, 1630. From Hakewill, who was Arch-
deacon of Surrey, and to whom Boswell gives
the credit of helping to form the style of Johnson, Walton probably got his information as to
Macrobius and Varro, the Roman aviaries, the
Roman fish-ponds, the serving-in of fish with
music, the account from Seneca of the dying
mullet, and the story of the lamprey that was
mourned by Hortensius the orator,—although

in this last case, Walton, while citing Hakewill as his authority, adds, after his fashion, a detail which Hakewill does not give, inasmuch as he says that Hortensius had kept the lamprey long. Another work to which Walton seems to have had actual access is the Rev. Edward Topsell's *Historie of Fowre-footed Beasts,* 1607. From Topsell he takes much of his description of the Otter at the beginning of his second chapter, and his easy method of borrowing has apparently been the means of burdening the language with a needless word. Topsell writes (p. 574) of a " kind of *Assa* called Benioyn," the smell of which drives away the Otter. The fragrant resin or gum intended is obviously that obtained from the Styrax benzoin of Sumatra and Java, popularly known as "benjamin." But under Walton's transforming pen, it becomes the " herb [?] *Benione,*" and Benione as an obsolete form of benzoin, forthwith takes its place in the New English Dictionary, with the sentence from the *Compleat Angler* for its *pièce justificative.*

One more illustration of the Waltonian method. In the fifth chapter of his fifth edition, p. 110, he represents the " devout Lessius " as saying—" That poor men, and those that fast often, have much more pleasure in eating than rich men and gluttons, that always feed before their stomachs are empty of their last meat, and call for more : for by that means they rob themselves of that pleasure that hunger brings to poor men." The Lessius referred to is Leonard Lessio or Lessius, sometime Professor of Divinity and Philosophy at the Jesuits' College of Louvain, whose *Hygiasticon, seu vera Ratio Valetudinis bonœ et Vitœ* was published at Antwerp in 1613, a second edition following in 1614. In 1634 it was translated into English by Timothy Smith, with the sub-title, *The right course of preserving Life and Health unto extream old Age ;* and to Smith's version, as to the tract of Lessius, was added a rendering of Lewis Cornaro's *Treatise of Temperance.* Lessius had made his own translation into Latin from Cornaro's Italian ; Smith's English version was by George Herbert. It is probable that, as Walton's editors suppose, this tiny 12mo, issued from Cambridge in the same year as the *Select Dialogues of Lucian* was issued at Oxford, must have been known to Walton. As far as we can ascertain, however, neither in Lessius nor Cornaro is there any passage corresponding to the above, although it may fairly be described as an inference from the teaching of both. And it is in italic type, just like Wharton's description, already mentioned, of the "strange fish."

It would no doubt be easy to give farther specimens of Walton's treatment of Sylvester's Du Bartas, of Peter Heylin, of Dubravius, Méric Casaubon, Cardanus, Paulus Jovius, and the rest of the worthies whose "highly respectable names" add weight to his pages. But what has been noted will suffice. The scantlings of learning with which he sought to dignify his book are no essential part of it ; and this desultory inquiry has certainly not been undertaken in the spirit or the interest of those "severe, sowre complexion'd" critics whom Walton, in his Address to the Reader, disallows to be competent judges of his performance. What we want most, no less, from this delightful author, is himself, not the "scattered sapience" derived at second hand and superficially from Dr. Wharton of Gresham College, or Dr. Sheldon of All Soul's, but the "right," neat, and unsophisticated Walton who "babbles of green fields," gossips of the haycocks and the soft May-rain, or copies down the ditty that *Maudlin* the milkmaid "sung last night, when young *Corydon* the Shepherd plaid so purely on his *oaten pipe* to her and her cozen Betty." It is this Walton we must have,—the Walton of the cheerful spirit and the clean morality,—of the frank old words that smell of the soil and the fresh-turned furrows. Rondeletius and Salvian and Aldrovandus and Gasper Peucerus no doubt served to astonish and impress " honest Nat. and R. Roe " while they waited in the parlour of the Thatched House at Hoddesdon, or the George at Ware, for the twenty-two inch trout whose belly, when taken, was " part of it as yellow as a marigold, and part of it as white as a lilly." But we—we prefer to sit with Father Izaak outside in the sweetbriar Arbour, discussing a bottle of the " *Sack, Milk, Oranges* and *Sugar*, which all put together, make a drink like *Nectar ;* " or to hear him repeat—probably with variations of his own—some sample of choicely good Verses made by that excellent Poet and Lover of *Angling* (now with God), Sir Henry Wotton, once Provost of Eton College.

"VADER CATS"

TO an uninstructed reader the homely name that heads this paper does not, in itself, suggest any special distinction. When we are informed that Jacob Cats was a native of Holland, our first impression is of some typical Dutchman, squat-figured and stolid, preoccupied with a pipe and tulips. If it be added that he wrote verses, speculation goes no farther than to conceive a minstrel of the type of Longfellow's " Cobbler of Hagenau," chirruping his songs at his work-bench, and having ever

> " at his side,
> Among his leathers and his tools,
> Reynard the Fox, the Ship of Fools,
> Or Eulenspiegel, open wide."

Each of these forecasts, however, is equally at fault. As a Dutchman, Jacob Cats was one of the prominent men of his age. He had gained honour as a Greek Scholar at Leyden University; he had travelled in France and England, visiting both Oxford and Cambridge. He was an accomplished jurist; and though—

as some authorities allege—he had but little success as a politician, he was, at all events, a great civic dignitary in the great days of the Netherlands, holding important office as a magistrate at Middleburgh and Dordrecht, and ultimately proceeding Grand Pensionary of Holland. He was twice Ambassador to England, being knighted on the first occasion by Charles I. When finally, at the age of seventy-two, he obtained the permission of the States to retire into private life at his country-seat of Sorgh-vliet—his "Sans-Souci" or "Castle-Careless"—on the Scheveningen Road, it was as a man who on the whole had deserved well of his generation, and might fairly be permitted to "cultivate his garden," and write his "Reminiscences."

But if he acquired a reputation as a citizen, he earned a still greater reputation as a poet. He was a contemporary of Hooft and Vondel, and that delightful Tesselschade Visscher, of whom Mr. Edmund Gosse has given us so pleasant a portrait;[1] and he was probably the most popular of the four. By his readers he was affectionately styled "Vader Cats"; and

---

[1] *Studies in the Literature of Northern Europe*, 1879, pp. 230-277.

his collected works in familiar moments were known as the " Household Bible." His big folio was to be found by poor men's hearths, and in the windows of the rich—even as Baker's "Chronicle" lay in the windows of Sir Roger de Coverley. When now we open the vast volume (*i. e.*, Jan Jacobz Schipper's Amsterdam edition of 1655), its bulk appals us. It is a book to be approached only from the side of dimension. It is so high : it measures so much about. Not to lay stress on the blackness of the type, which is in itself portentous, it is printed in two columns,—sometimes even in three. Turning the tall pages timidly, you become conscious, in addition to a Babel of proverbs and emblems in all languages, of a long didactic poem on "Marriage" (*Houwelick*), which traces that institution, with abundant illustration, from maidenhood to widowhood. Then of another, and a still longer effort, entitled "Nuptial Ring" (*Trou-ringh*), wherein it is treated, amongst other things, of Crates and Hipparchia, of Adam and Eve, of Masinissa and Sophonisba, of Eginhard and the daughter of Charlemagne, of Jacob and Rachel. (Jacob, it may be noted in parenthesis, has apparently been educated in France, for in the picture he has carved "la belle Rachell" upon a tree-trunk, and written under it " Vive l'Amour"). Then there is a " pastoral romance " of " Galatea"; a poem on " Country-Life " (*Buytenleven*), in the frontispiece of which is a view of Sorgh-vliet, and towards the end of the book, another series of poems called cheerfully " Coffins for the Living " (*Doodt-Kiste voor de Levendige*). These are only part of the contents. Beside and between them are numerous other pieces, accompanied like the rest by prefaces and sub-prefaces, by appendices, excursuses, commentaries, head-notes, shoulder-notes, sidenotes, foot-notes, postscripts, and addresses to the *Lector benignus* (*"goetgunstige Leser"*) which hedge them in on all sides. Poetry, with this Dutch poet, is not by any means a trickling rill from Helicon; it is an inundation *à la mode du pays*,—a flood in a flat land, covering everything far and near with its sluggish waters.

To this immoderate and incontinent effusiveness is probably to be attributed the fact that, notwithstanding their excellent precepts and praiseworthy morality, the poems of Jacob Cats do not seem to have largely attracted the translator. Report, indeed, affirms that his entire works have been " done into German "; but this would be of little service to the ordinary

English reader.   The French, on the other
hand, have contented themselves with an imitation of the short piece entitled "Children's
Games" (*Kinder-Spel*).   In our own country,
multifarious old Thomas Heywood, the drama-
tist, paraphrased the first part of *Houwelick*
under the title of "An Emblematicall Dialogue,
interpreted from the excellent and most learned
D. Jac. Catʒius; which showeth how Virgins
in their chaste loves ought to bear themselves."
And as late as 1860 many of the emblems and
proverbs were translated by Richard Pigot to
accompany the "freely-rendered" cuts of John
Leighton.   But our concern here is less with
the text than with the old copper-plates which
originally accompanied it, and which, fortunately for us, speak a universal language.

These, printed in the body of the page, are
generally uniform in size, and surrounded by a
conventional border.   Many of them bear the
initials or names of such well-known engravers
as Hondius, the two Mathams, and Crispin van
Queborn.   But the main interest centres in the
chief designer, Adrian van der Venne, a painter
of considerable ability, and noted especially for
the prodigious canvases on which, like the
Frenchman Lebrun, he depicted the battles of
the seventeenth century.   After drifting to and

fro, he seems to have settled at Middleburgh,
where Cats also resided from 1602 to 1620.
His brother, Jan Pietersz van der Venne, was
a bookseller and publisher of the town, and for
him he executed numberless book-illustrations
in addition to those now under consideration.
He is said also to have possessed no mean
literary talent, and to have written satirical
works.　It is probably a natural consequence
of his *modus operandi* that he should reproduce
his environment ; and many views and memories
of the capital of Zeeland and the surrounding
country are traceable in his compositions.　Perhaps the most interesting of these is to be found
in the large head-piece to the above-mentioned
" Children's Games," the background of which
exhibits the great square of Middleburgh, with
its old Gothic houses and central clump of trees.
This is, moreover, as delightful a picture as any
in the gallery.　Down the middle of the fore-
ground, which is filled by a crowd of figures,
advances a regiment of little Dutchmen, marching to drum and fife, and led by a fire-eating
captain of fifteen.　Around this central group
are dispersed knots of children, playing leap-
frog, flying kites, blowing bubbles, whipping
tops, walking on stilts, skipping and the like.
In one corner the boys are busy with blind

man's buff ; in the other the girls, with their
stiff head-dresses and vandyked aprons, are occupied with their dolls.   Under the pump some
seventeenth-century equivalent for chuck-far-
thing seems to be going on vigorously ; and, not
to be behindhand in the fun, two little fellows
in the distance are standing upon their heads.
The whole composition is full of life and move-
ment, and—so conservative is childhood—
might, but for the costume and scene, represent
a playground of to-day.   No doubt it represented, with far closer fidelity, the playground
of the artist's time.

It is this note of literalness—this truth to
what lay nearest—that constitutes the chief
charm of these illustrations.   Many of those to
the " Emblems " are quaint with that inventive
strangeness and naïve ingenuity which have a
fascination apart from technical merit.   But, as
a rule, the artist is strongest in what he has
seen.   His lions are more or less heraldic ; his
crocodiles are badly stuffed ; and his sala-
manders of doubtful actuality.   There is no
such faltering when he shows us a hammer
striking a flint on a cushion, or a pair of snuffers
cropping a candle, or the interior of a black-
smith's shop.   What applies to the still-life applies equally to the figures.   When the subject

is a tailor sitting cross-legged in his stall, or a
woman warming her feet and gazing into the
embers, there is no doubt of the reality of the
studies. Some of them, indeed, are finished
works in *genre*.

What would one not give for such an illustrated copy of Shakespeare! In these pages of
Jacob Cats we have the authentic Holland of
the seventeenth century :—its vanes and spires
and steep-roofed houses ; its gardens with their
geometric tulip-beds, their formally-clipped
alleys and arches, their shining parallelograms
of water. Here are its old-fashioned interiors,
with the deep fireplaces and queer andirons, the
huge four-posters, the prim portraits on the
wall, the great brass-clamped coffers and carved
armoires for the ruffs and starched collars and
stiff farthingales of the women. In one picture
you may see the careful housewife mournfully
inspecting a moth-eaten garment which she has
just taken from a chest that Wardour Street
might envy ; in another she is energetically
cuffing the " foolish fat scullion," who has let
the spotted coach-dog overturn the cauldron at
the fire. Here an old crone, with her spectacles
on, is cautiously probing the contents of the
said cauldron with a fork ; here the mistress of
the house is peeling pears ; here the plump and

soft-hearted cheese-wife is entertaining an admirer. Outside there are pictures as vivid. Here are the clumsy leather-topped coach with its masked occupant and stumbling horses ; the towed *trekschuit*, with its merry freight, sliding swiftly through the low-lying landscape; the windy mole, stretching seaward, with its flaring beacon-fire. Here again in the street is the toy-shop with its open front and store of mimic drums and halberds for the martial little burghers ; here are the fruiteress with her stall of grapes and melons, the rat-catcher with his string of trophies, the fowler and his clap-net, the furrier with his stock of skins. Many of the designs have also that additional interest which is universal as well as local. Such is the one to the proverb, "Between two stools one comes to the ground," or, as Cats has it " Nemo potest Thetidem simul et Galatean amare." The luckless Philander of the story has been trying to solve the problem, but without success. He has been flirting among the sand-hills with Thetis, who has her fish upon her head in "ocean-smelling osier"; and now Galatea the milkmaid has come suddenly upon them in a hat which looks like an inverted basin with a tuft : and he will probably experience what is high-Dutch for a *mauvais quart d'heure*.

Another illustrates as pertinently the adage, " It is ill hunting with unwilling hounds," although the dogs are but a detail in the landscape, and the real moral is pointed by humanity. " Griet," poor soul, shamefaced and ill-at-ease, stands awkwardly by the door-settle, looking away from the other actors in the drama, apparently her suitor and his father. By the purse in her hand we must conclude she is rich ; by a certain constraint in her carriage we may perhaps also infer that she is not so well-born as her intended. It is, in fact, a Batavian "marriage *à la mode*" that is in progress, if such a word may be employed where nothing is progressing. For if the lady is simply passive, the gentleman, whose name is Claes, is violently demonstrative. He resists all efforts of his senior to bring him to the front—gesticulates wildly, and digs his right heel doggedly in the ground. He will none of her, nor all her " brooches, pearls and owches,"—her gear and household stuff,—her rents and her comings-in.

The round cap and collar of the female figure in this picture, the short-skirt with its rigid folds and dark border, the puffed shoulder-pieces and long chatelaine, remind us of one characteristic of these designs which might be anticipated in so observant an artist, but which not the less deserves especial mention. This is the excellence and variety of the costume. And it is not only the peasants and fish-women whose dress is faithfully reproduced, but that of the better classes is as scrupulously delineated. It would take a chapter to describe the wonderful cavaliers, with their long-plumed hats and slashed jerkins, their endless tags and aiglets and rosettes; or the sumptuous ladies with their broidered sleeves, and purfled stomachers, and monumental ruffs. The design inscribed " Amor, 'ut pila, vices exigit," which may be roughly Englished by " Love asks return," is an example of this, which is as good as any. In a " trim garden," with symmetrically-clipped trees and hedges, a gentleman and a lady are playing at battledore and shuttlecock. The former, whose right foot is neatly turned out after the most approved fashion, so as to show the inside of his calf, has just delivered his blow ; the latter leaps lightly to return it with as much agility as may be consistent with good manners and a buckramed state attire.

There is also a certain grim side to these Dutch moralities which is not without its significance. Through the whole series it peeps out here and there ; but it is more plainly manifest in the later works, when we must suppose old age to be stealing upon the writer, and busying his thoughts with Calvinistic images of mortality and decay. The illustration to one of these—a full-page plate—is certainly a most gruesome allegory of life. A man is seen scaling an apple-tree, which clings with snake-like roots to the side of a flaming pit or well, inhabited by a fearsome and ravening dragon. About the brim of the pit a restless bear runs backwards and forwards, eager for its prey; but rats are gnawing busily at the tree-trunk, and by and by the tree, climber and all, will topple crashing in the flames. Another composition—the frontispiece to " Coffins for the Living "—takes up two pages, and is even more impressive. The scene is a kind of cemetery with magnificent sepulchral monuments, wherefrom the covers have been lifted so as to exhibit their mouldering tenants. To the right a party of richly-clad Orientals are gazing curiously at a crowned skeleton:—" Where are the riches of Crœsus?" On the opposite side of the picture, a personage resembling an Eastern Mage, and a beautiful and majestic woman—perhaps the Queen of Sheba—bend wonderingly over a second tomb:—" Where is the wisdom of Solomon?" Here it is a group of soldiers that is attracted; there a group of

heroes. But the main interest centres in front
of a lofty canopy, the sable curtains of which
are drawn aside by grinning atomies, discover-
ing a figure more pitiful than any in its forlorn
and fleshless impotence :—" Where is the
beauty of Helen?" "Was *this* the face that
launch'd a thousand ships, and burned the top-
less towers of Ilium?" Surely a fruitful theme
for the gray-haired sage of Sorgh-vliet, when the
blast whistled keener through his wind-stripped
espaliers, and the dead leaves gathered at the
garden borders!

And here we close the great folio. But what
a picture-book it must have been in the days
when picture books were fewer! One can imagine the Dutch children poring over it, much
as Charles Lamb pored over the queer illustrations in Stackhouse's " History of the Bible."
One can even fancy that their minds took a certain haunting after-colour or savour from this
early study, like the jar which, as Horace says,
remembers its first wine. That the volume is a
favourite with the distinguished Dutch artist,
now naturalised among us, Sir Laurence Alma-
Tadema, is, perhaps, not remarkable ; nor is it
remarkable that (as Mr. Warter relates) it
should have attracted the wandering and omniv-
orous appetite of Southey. But it is surely of

special interest that it was among the first art-treasures of Reynolds, who loved it as a boy, and many of whose sketches—" done by Joshua out of pure idleness "—were copied from the gallery of "Vader Cats. "

PART II.

OCCASIONAL VERSES AND INSCRIPTIONS.

(Too hard it is to sing
  In these untuneful times,
When only coin can ring,
  And no one cares for rhymes !

Alas ! for him who climbs
  To Aganippe's spring :—
Too hard it is to sing
In these untuneful times !

His kindred clip his wing ;
  His feet the critic limes ;
If Fame her laurel bring
  Old Age his forehead rimes :—
Too hard it is to sing
  In these untuneful times !)

A BALLAD OF THE QUEEN'S MAJESTY.

(June 22, 1897.)

NAME that has been thy nation's shield
   On many an alien shore and sea ;
Name that in many a fateful field
   Has taught the stubborn foe to flee ;
   Promise and proof of virtues three,
Valour unvaunting, vigour, verve,
   We hail thy white-winged Sovereignty,
VICTORIA !—WHOM GOD PRESERVE !

Monarchs there are to whom men yield
   Obeisance—in a bondman's key ;
Monarchs whose sceptred might doth wield
   Only the rod of Tyranny ;
   We, in free homage, being free,—
We joy that naught can shake or curve
   Thy rectitude of Royalty,
VICTORIA !—WHOM GOD PRESERVE !

Therefore from all our towers be pealed
   The note of greeting ; therefore be,
As from a thousand springs unsealed,
   Outpoured the tide of mirth and glee ;
   For surely not to-day shall we

From sixty years' allegiance swerve,
  Or shame thy twice-told Jubilee,
VICTORIA !—WHOM GOD PRESERVE !

ENVOY.

QUEEN !—to whom true men bend the knee,
  Our island heart and brain and nerve.
Are loyal—loyal unto thee,
  VICTORIA !—WHOM GOD PRESERVE !

A MADRIGAL.

(Written for " Choral Songs in Honour of Queen
Victoria," 1899.)

I.

WHO can dwell with greatness ! Greatness
is too high ;
Flowers are for the meadow, suns are for the
sky ;—
Ah ! but there is greatness in this land of ours,
High as is the sunlight, humble as the flowers !

II.

Queen, of thee the fable ! Lady, thine the fate !
Royal, and yet lowly, lowly and yet great ;—
Great in far dominion, great in bannered years,
Greater still as woman, greatest in thy tears !

FOR A FLORAL WREATH.

(January 22, 1901.)

GREAT Queen, great Lady, Mother most of
    all !
Beyond the turmoil of Earth's hopes and
    fears,
How should you need the tribute of our
    tears ?—
Our helpless, useless tears !   But they must fall.

RANK AND FILE.

(South Africa, 1900–1.)

I.

O UNDISTINGUISHED Dead !
  Whom the bent covers, or the rock-
    strewn steep
Shows to the stars, for you I mourn,—I weep,
  O undistinguished Dead !

II.

  None knows your name.
Blacken'd and blurr'd in the wild battle's brunt,
Hotly you fell . . . with all your wounds in
    front ;
  This is your fame !

A POSTSCRIPT TO GOLDSMITH'S
"RETALIATION."

[*After the Fourth Edition of* DOCTOR GOLD-
SMITH'S RETALIATION *was printed, the Publisher
received a supplementary Epitaph on the Wit and
Punster* CALEB WHITEFOORD. *Though it is
found appended to the later issues of the Poem, it
has been suspected that* WHITEFOORD *wrote it
himself. It may be that the following, which
has recently come to light, is another forgery.*]

HERE JOHNSON is laid.   Have a care how
you walk ;
If he stir in his sleep, in his sleep he will talk.
Ye gods ! how he talk'd ! What a torrent of
sound,
His hearers invaded, encompass'd and—drown'd!
What a banquet of memory, fact, illustration,
In that innings-for-one that he called *conversa-
tion !*
Can't you hear his sonorous " Why no, Sir ! "
and " Stay, Sir !
Your premiss is wrong," or " You don't see
your way, Sir ! "

How he silenc'd a prig, or a slip-shod romancer !
How he pounc'd on a fool with a knock-me-
    down answer !

But peace to his slumbers !   Tho' rough in the
    rind,
The heart of the giant was gentle and kind :
What signifies now, if in bouts with a friend,
When his pistol miss'd fire, he would use the
    butt-end ?
If he trampled your flow'rs, like a bull in a
    garden,
What matter for that ? he was sure to ask par-
    don ;
And you felt on the whole, tho' he'd toss'd you
    and gor'd you,
It was something, at least, that he had not
    ignor'd you.
Yes ! the outside was rugged.   But test him
    within,
You found he had nought of the bear but the
    skin ;
And for bottom and base to his *anfractuosity*,
A fund of fine feeling, good taste, generosity.
He was true to his conscience, his King, and
    his duty ;
And he hated the *Whigs*, and he soften'd to
    Beauty.

Turn now to his Writings.   I grant, in his tales,
That he made little fishes talk vastly like whales;
I grant that his language was rather emphatic,
Nay, even—to put the thing plainly—dogmatic;
But read him for Style,—and dismiss from your
     thoughts,
The crowd of compilers who copied his faults,—
Say, where is there English so full and so clear,
So weighty, so dignified, manly, sincere?
So strong in expression, conviction, persuasion?
So prompt to take colour from place and occa-
     sion?
So widely remov'd from the doubtful, the tenta-
     tive;
So truly—and in the best sense—argumentative?
You may talk of your BURKES and your GIBBONS
     so clever,
But I hark back to him with a " JOHNSON for-
     ever ! "
And I feel as I muse on his ponderous figure,
Tho' he's great in this age, in the next he'll
     grow bigger;
And still while . . .   [*Cœtera Desunt.*]

VERSES READ AT THE DINNER OF THE OMAR KHAYYÁM CLUB ON THURSDAY, MARCH 25, 1897.

" —Medio de fonte leporum
Surgit OMARI *aliquid."*
—LUCRETIUS (*adapted*).

While we the Feast by Fruit and Wine prolong,
A Bard bobs up, and bores us with a Song.
—THE APICIAD.

'TWAS SWIFT who said that people " view
   In HOMER more than HOMER knew."
I can't pretend to claim the gift
Of playing BENTLEY upon SWIFT ;
But I suspect the reading true
Is " OMAR more than OMAR knew,"—
Or why this large assembly met
Lest we this OMAR should forget ?
(In a parenthesis I note
Our RUSTUM here, without red coat ;
Where SOHRAB sits I'm not aware,
But that's FIRDAUSI in the chair !)—
I say then that we now are met
Lest we this OMAR should forget,

Who, ages back, remote, obscure,
Wrote verses once at Naishápúr,—
Verses which, as I understand,
Were merely copied out by hand,
And now, without etched plates, or aid
Of India paper, or handmade,
Bid fair Parnassus' top to climb,
And knock the Classics out of time.

Persicos odi—Horace said,
And therefore is no longer read.
Time, who could simply not endure
Slight to the Bard of Naishápúr,
(Time, by the way, was rather late
For one so often up-to-date !)
Went swiftly to the Roll of Fame
And blotted Q. H. F. his name,
Since when, for every youth or miss
That knows *Quis multa gracilis*,
There are a hundred who can tell
What OMAR thought of Heav'n and Hell;
Who BAHRÁM was ; and where (at need)
Lies hid the Beaker of JAMSHYD ;—
In short, without a break can quote
Most of what OMAR ever wrote.

Well, OMAR KHAYYÁM wrote of Wine,
And all of us, sometimes, must dine ;

And OMAR KHAYYÁM wrote of Roses,
And all of us, no doubt, have noses;
And OMAR KHAYYÁM wrote of Love,
Which some of us are not above.
Also, he charms to this extent,
We don't know, always, what he meant.
Lastly, the man's so plainly dead
We can heap honours on his head.

Then, too, he scores in other wise
By his "deplorable demise."
There is so much that we could say
Were he a Bard of yesterday!
We should discuss his draughts and pills,
His baker's and his vintner's bills;
Rake up—perhaps 'tis well we can't—
Gossip about his maiden aunt;
And all that marketable matter
Which FREEMAN nicknamed " Harriet-chatter!"
But here not even Persian candles
Can light us to the smallest scandals;—
Thus far your OMAR gains at least
By having been so long deceased.

Failing of this, we needs must fall
Back on his *opus* after all;—
Those quatrains so compact, complete,
So suited to FITZGERALD's feet,

(And, let us add, so subtly planned
To tempt the imitative band!)—
Those censers of *Omari* ware
That breathe into the perfumed air   }
His doubt, his unrest, his despair ;—
Those jewels-four-lines-long that show,
Eight hundred years and more ago,
An old thing underneath the sun
In Babylonish Babylon :—
A Body and a Soul at strife
To solve the Mystery of Life !

So then all hail to OMAR K.!
(To take our more familiar way)
Though much of what he wrote and did
In darkest mystery is hid ;
And though (unlike our bards) his task
Was less to answer than to ask ;
For all his endless Why and Whether,
He brings us here to-night together ;
And therefore (as I said before),
Hail ! OMAR KHAYYÁM, hail ! once more !

FOR A COPY OF "THE COMPLEAT ANGLER."

" *Le rêve de la vie champêtre a été de tout temps l'idéal des villes.*"—GEORGE SAND.

I CARE not much how folk prefer
  To dress your *Chubb* or *Chavender ;*—
I care no whit for line or hook,
But still I love old IZAAK's book,
Wherein a man may read at ease
Of " gander-grass " and " culver-keys,"
Or with half-pitying wonder, note
What *Topsell*, what *Du Bartas* wrote,
Or list the song, by *Maudlin* sung,
That *Marlowe* made when he was young :—
These things, in truth, delight me more
Than all old IZAAK's angling lore.

These were his Secret. What care I
How men concoct the Hawthorn-fly,
Who could as soon make Syllabub
As catch your *Chavender* or *Chubb ;*
And might not, in ten years, arrive
At baiting hooks with frogs, alive !—
But still I love old IZAAK's page,

Old IZAAK's simple *Golden Age*,
Where blackbirds flute from ev'ry bough,
Where lasses " milk the sand-red cow,"
Where lads are " sturdy foot ball swains,"
And nought but soft " May-butter " rains ;—
Where you may breathe untainted air
Either at *Hodsden* or at *Ware ;*
And sing, or slumber, or look wise
Till *Phœbus* sink adown the skies ;
Then, laying rod and tackle by,
Choose out some " cleanly Alehouse " nigh,
With ballads " stuck about the wall,"
Of *Joan of France* or *English Mall* —
With sheets that smell of lavender —
There eat your *Chubb* (or *Chavender*),
And keep old IZAAK's honest laws
For " mirth that no repenting draws "—
To wit, a friendly stave or so,
That goes to *Heigh-trolollie-loe*
Or more to make the ale-can pass,
A hunting song of *William Basse* —
Then talk of fish and fishy diet,
And dream you " Study to be quiet."

THE COLLECTOR TO HIS LIBRARY.

(Written for Ballads of Books, 1887.)

BROWN Books of mine, who never yet
Have caused me anguish or regret,—
Save when some fiend in human shape
Has set your tender sides agape,
Or soiled with some unmanly smear
The candour of your margin clear,
Or writ you with some phrase inane,
The bantling of an idle brain,—
I love you: and because must end
This commerce between friend and friend,
I do implore each kindly Fate—
To each and all I supplicate—
That you, whom I have loved so long,
May not be vended " for a song ";—
That you, my dear desire and care,
May 'scape the common thoroughfare,
The dust, the eating rain, and all
The shame and squalor of the Stall.
Rather I trust your lot may touch
Some Crœsus—if there should be such—

To buy you, and that you may so
From Crœsus unto Crœsus go
Till that inevitable day
When comes your moment of decay.

This, more than other good, I pray.

FOR "AN APPENDIX TO THE ROW-FANT LIBRARY."

(F. L. L. : In Memoriam.)

"HIS Books." Oh yes, his Books I
     know,—
Each worth a monarch's ransom ;
But now, beside their row on row,
    I see, erect and handsome,

The courtly Owner, glass in eye,
    With half-sad smile, forerunning
Some triumph of an apt reply,—
    Some master-stroke of punning.

Where shall we meet his like again ?
    Where hear, in such perfection,
Such genial talk of gods and men,—
    Such store of recollection ;

Or where discern a verse so neat,
    So well-bred and so witty,—
So finished in its least conceit,
    So mixed of mirth and pity ?

POPE taught him rhythm, PRIOR ease,
　PRAED buoyancy and banter ;
What modern bard would learn from these ?
　Ah, *tempora mutantur !*

The old *régime* departs,—departs ;
　Our days of mime and mocker,
For all their imitative arts,
　Produce no FREDERICK LOCKER.

"GOOD LUCK TO YOUR FISHING!"
(For a Picture by G. F. Watts, R. A.)

GOOD luck to your fishing !
     And what have you caught ?
Ah, would that my wishing
     Were more than a thought !
Ah, would you had caught her,
     Young Chloe, for me,—
Young Chloe, the daughter
     Of Proteus, the sea !

She irks me, she irks me,
     With blue of her eyes ;
She irks me, she irks me,
     With little drawn sighs ;
She lures me with laughter,
     She tempts me with tears ;
And hope follows after,—
     Hope only,—and fears !

Good luck to your fishing !
     But would you had caught
That maid beyond wishing,
     That maid beyond thought !
O cast the line deeper,
     Deep—deep in the sea ;
And catch her, and keep her,
     Dan Cupid, for me !

"WHEN THIS OLD WORLD WAS NEW."

(For a Lady's Autograph-Book.)

WHEN this old world was new,
    Before the towns were made,
Love was a shepherd too.

Clear-eyed as flowers men grew,
Of evil unafraid,
When this old world was new.

No skill had they to woo,
Who but their hearts obey'd —
Love was a shepherd too.

What need to feign or sue !
Not so was life delay'd
When this old world was new.

Under the candid blue
They kiss'd their shepherd-maid —
Love was a shepherd too.

They knew but joy ; they knew
No whit of state or grade :
When this old world was new,
Love was a shepherd too.

FOR A COPY OF THE "VICAR OF WAKEFIELD."

BY GOLDSMITH's tomb, the City's cry
   Grows faint and distant ; now no more,
From that famed Street he trod of yore,
Men turn where those old Templars lie !
Only some dreamer such as I
   Pauses awhile from dust and roar
             By GOLDSMITH's tomb !

And then—ah, then ! when none is nigh,
   What shadowy shapes, unseen before,
   Troop back again from Lethe's shore ! —
How the ghosts gather then, and sigh
             By GOLDSMITH's tomb !

AFTER A HOLIDAY.

THREE little ducks by a door,
    Snuggling aside in the sun;
The sweep of a threshing-floor,
    A flail with its One-two, One;

A shaggy-haired, loose-limbed mare,
    Grave as a master at class;
A foal with its heels in the air,
    Rolling, for joy, in the grass;

A sunny-eyed, golden-haired lad,
    Laughing, astride on a wall;
A collie-dog, lazily glad . . .
    Why do I think of it all?

Why? From my window I see,
    Once more through the dust-dry pane
The sky like a great Dead Sea,
    And the lash of the London rain;

And I read—here in London town,
    Of a murder done at my gate,
And a goodly ship gone down,
    And of homes made desolate;

And I know, with the old sick heart,
  That but for a moment's space,
We may shut our sense, and part
  From the pain of this tarrying place.

FOR A CHARITY ANNUAL.

IN Angel-Court the sunless air
   Grows faint and sick ; to left and right
The cowering houses shrink from sight,
Huddling and hopeless, eyeless, bare.

Misnamed, you say ?   For surely rare
   Must be the angel-shapes that light
             In Angel-Court !

Nay !—the Eternities are there.
   Death at the doorway stands to smite ;
   Life in its garrets leaps to light ;
And Love has climbed that crumbling stair
             In Angel-Court.

ON A PICTURE BY HOPPNER.

(Mrs. Gwyn,—Goldsmith's "Jessamy Bride.")

" AND you went once with myrtle crowned ! "
    You once were she, for whom
Poor GOLDSMITH's gentle genius found
    That name of jasmine-bloom !

How strange it seems ! You whom he loved,
    You who were breathing,—vital,—
Not feigned in books,—for us have proved
    Scarce but a fragrant title ;—

A shape too shadowy far to stand
    Beside the girl PRIMROSES,—
Beside the dear old VICAR, and
    Our more-than-brother, MOSES !

We cannot guess your voice, who know
    Scamp Tony's view-halloo ;
For us e'en thin Beau Tibbs must show
    More palpable than you !—

Yet some scant news we have.   You came,
  When that kind soul had fled ;
You begged his hair ; you kept his name
  Long on your lips, 'tis said ;

You lived ;—and died.   Or when, or how,
  Who asks !   This age of ours
But marks your grass-grown headstone now
  GOLDSMITH's jasmine flowers !

THE PHILOSOPHY OF THE PORCH.

BY A SUMMER-DAY STOIC.

(To A. J. MUNBY.)

" Cultivous notre jardin."
—VOLTAIRE.

A CROSS my Neighbour's waste of whins
　　For roods the rabbit burrows ;
You scarce can see where first begins
　　His range of steaming furrows ;
I am not sad that he is great,
　　He does not ask my pardon ;
Beside his wall I cultivate
　　My modest patch of garden.

I envy not my Neighbour's trees ;—
　　To me it nowise matters
Whether in east or western breeze
　　His " dry-tongued laurel patters."
Me too the bays become ; but still,
　　I sleep without narcotics,
Though he should bind his brows at will
　　With odorous exotics.

Let Goodman Greenfat, glad to dine,
  With true *bon-vivant's* benison,
Extol my Neighbour's wit and wine,—
  His virtue and his venison :
I care not.   Still for me the gorse
  Will blaze about the thicket ;
The Common's purblind pauper horse
  Will peer across my wicket ;

For me the geese will thread the furze,
  In hissing file, to follow
The tinker's sputtering wheel that whirs
  Across the breezy hollow ;
And look, where smoke of gipsy huts
  Curls blue against the bushes,—
That little copse is famed for nuts,
  For nightingales and thrushes !

But hark !   I hear my Neighbour's drums !
  Some dreary deputation
Of Malice or of Wonder comes
  In guise of Adulation.
Poor Neighbour !   Though you like the tune,
  One little pinch of care is
Enough to clog a whole balloon
  Of *aura popularis ;*

Not amulets, nor epiderm
   As tough as armadillo's,
Can shield you if Suspicion worm
   Between your easy pillows ;
And, though on ortolans you sup,
   Beside you shadowy sitters
Can pour in your ungenial cup
   Unstimulating bitters.

Let Envy crave, and Avarice save ;
   Let Folly ride her circuit ;
I hold that—on this side the grave —
   To find one's vein and work it,
To keep one's wants both fit and few,
   To cringe to no condition,
To count a candid friend or two,—
   May bound a man's ambition.

Swell, South-wind, swell my Neighbour's sails ;
   Fill, Fortune, fill his coffers ;
If Fate has made his *rôle* the whale's,
   And we the minnow's offers ;
I am not sad that he is great,
   He need not ask my pardon ;
Beside his wall I cultivate
   My modest patch of garden.

THE HOLOCAUST.

" Heart-free, with the least little touch of spleen."
—MAUD.

ABOVE my mantelshelf there stands
　　A little, bronze sarcophagus,
Carved by its unknown artist's hands,
　　With this one word—AMORIBUS !

Along the lid a Love lies dead :
　　Across his breast his broken bow ;
Elsewhere they dig his tiny bed,
　　And round it women wailing go :—

A trick, a toy—mere " Paris ware,"
　　Some Quartier-Latin sculptor's whim,
Wrought in a fit of mock despair,
　　With sight, it may be something dim,

Because the love of yesterday,
　　Had left the *grenier*, light MUSETTE,
And she who made the morrow gay,
　　LUTINE or MIMI, was not yet,—

A toy. But ah ! what hopes deferred,
  (O friend, with sympathetic eye !)
What vows (now decently interred)
  Within that " narrow compass " lie !

For there, last night, not sadly, too,
  With one live ember I cremated
A nest of cooing *billets-doux*,
  That just two decades back were dated.

THE STREET SINGER.

(For "Walnuts and Wine.")

H E stands at the curb and sings,
    'Tis a doleful tune and slow . . .
Ah me, if I had but wings!

He bends to the coin one flings,
But he never attempts to go,—
He stands at the curb, and sings.

The conjurer comes with his rings,
And the Punch-and-Judy show.
(Ah me, if I had but wings!)

They pass, like all fugitive things,—
They fade and they pass, but lo!
He stands at the curb and sings.

All the magic that music brings
Is lost when he murders it so . . .
Ah me! if I had but wings!

But the worst is a thought that stings,
There is nothing at hand to throw,—
He stands at the curb and sings . . .
Ah me! if I had but wings!

THE BALLAD OF THE BORE.

(For " Alma Mater's Mirror," 1887.)

" *Garrulus hunc quando consumet cunque.*"
—Hor. Sat. ix, lib. i.

I SEE him come from far,
   And, sick with hopelessness,
Invoke some kindly star,—
   I see him come, not less.
   Is there no sure recess
Where hunted men may lie?
   Ye Gods, it is too hard!
I feel his glittering eye,—
   Defend us from The Bard!

He knows nor let nor bar:
   With ever-nearing stress,
Like Juggernaut his car,
   I see him onward press;
   He waves a huge MS. ;
He puts evasion by,
   He stands—as one on guard,
And reads—how volubly!—
   Defend us from The Bard!

He reads—of Fates that mar,
  Of Woes beyond redress,
Of all the Moons that are,
  Of maids that never bless
  (As one, indeed, might guess);
Of Vows, of Hopes too high,
  Of Dolours by the yard
That none believe (nor buy),—
  Defend us from The Bard!

ENVOY.

PRINCE PHŒBUS, all must die,
  Or well- or evil-starred,
  Or whole of heart or scarred;
But why in this way—why?
  Defend us from The Bard.

JULY.

(Virelai Nouveau.)

G OOD-BYE to the Town!—good-bye!
Hurrah! for the sea and the sky!

In the street the flower-girls cry;
In the street the water-carts ply;
And a fluter, with features awry,
Plays fitfully, "Scots wha hae"—
And the throat of that fluter is dry;—
Good-bye to the Town!—good-bye!

And over the roof-tops nigh
Comes a waft like a dream of the May;
And a lady-bird lit on my tie;
And a cock-chafer came with the tray;
And a butterfly (no one knows why)
Mistook my Aunt's cap for a spray;
And "next door" and "over the way"
The neighbours take wing and fly:—
Hurrah for the sea and the sky!

To Buxton, the waters to try,—
To Buxton goes old Mrs. Bligh;
And the Captain to Homburg and play
Will carry his cane and his eye;

And even Miss Morgan Lefay
Is flitting—to far Peckham Rye ;
And my Grocer has gone—in a " Shay,"
And my Tailor has gone—in a " Fly ";—
Good-bye to the Town !—good-bye !

And it's O for the sea and the sky !
And it's O for the boat and the bay !
For the white foam whirling by,
And the sharp, salt edge of the spray !
For the wharf where the black nets fry,
And the wrack and the oarweed sway !
For the stroll when the moon is high
To the nook by the Flag-house gray !
For the *risus ab angulo* shy
From the Some-one we designate " Di ! "
For the moment of silence,—the sigh !
" How I *dote* on a Moon ! "　" So do I ! "
For the token we snatch on the sly !
(With nobody there to say Fie !)—
Hurrah ! for the sea and the sky !

So Phillis, the fawn-footed, hie
For a hansom.　Ere close of the **day**
Between us a " world " must lie,—
Good-bye to the Town !—Good-bye !
Hurrah ! for the sea and the sky !

NOTES OF A HONEYMOON.

*" Dans ce ravissant opéra qu'on appelle l'amour,
le libretto n'est presque rien."*
—Victor Hugo.

IN THE TRAIN.

AT last we are free,—
    All hail, Hymenæus !
From C, and from D,—
At last !—we are free.
What a comfort 'twill be
    " Mrs. Grundy" can't see us !
At last we are free,—
    All hail, Hymenæus !

FROM THE HOTEL WINDOW.

"What a mountain ! " " What ferns ! "
" And a pond, too, for Rover ! "
Da capo—in turns.
" What a mountain ! " " What ferns ! "
Meanwhile the toast burns,
    And the kettle boils over ;—
" What a mountain ! " " What ferns ! "
" And a pond, too, for Rover."

THE FIRST WALK.

" Join hands for a peep.
  You must keep yourself steady.
See the cliff goes down steep,—
Join hands for a peep.
This they call ' Lovers' Leap,'—
  We have leaped it already !
Join hands for a peep.
  You must keep yourself steady ! "

ARCADIA.

" I can hear a sheep-bell."
  " There are doves cooing yonder."
" It sounds like a spell,—
I can hear a sheep-bell."
" Shall we like this as well—
  In a twelvemonth ?"   " *I wonder !* "
" I can hear a sheep-bell."
  " There are doves cooing yonder."

AT A BOOKSTALL.

" Here it is in the ' Times,'—
  Dear Charlie,—how funny !
'Twixt a ' Smith ' and a ' Symes,'—
Here it is !—in the ' Times.' "

" And it's *not* with the ' crimes ' ! "
" You must pay. *I've* no money !
Here it is in the ' Times,'—
Dear Charlie,—how funny ! "

MISGIVINGS (No. 1).

" Poor Papa,—he's alone ! "
    She is sure he must miss her.
There's a tear in the tone,—
" *Poor* Papa ! *He's* alone ! "
At this point, I own,
    There is naught but to kiss her.
" Poor Papa,—he's alone ! "
    She is sure he must miss her.

MISGIVINGS (No. 2).

By-play as before.
    " Then you'll love me for ever ? "
" For ever—and more ! "
(By-play as before.)
" Never think me a ' bore ' ?—
    Never laugh at me ? "   "Never !! "
By-play as before.
    " Then you'll love me for ever ? "

THE SUM TOTAL.

She is all that is sweet !
   I must learn to deserve her.
Bright, kind . . . I repeat —
She is all that is sweet !
(Here a noise in the street
   Puts an end to my fervour.)
She is all that is sweet !
   I must learn to deserve her.

" CHANGE."

FREEZE, freeze, O icy wind !
 LUCILLA's cap's awry ;
No signal undesigned
 To those that read the sky.

Dull drags the breakfast by :
 She's something on her mind ;—
 Freeze, freeze, O icy wind !
LUCILLA's cap's awry !

" You're tired —" " And you're unkind ! "
 " You're cross —" " That I deny ! "
" Perhaps you're both combined."
 " I'm tired of You.—Good-bye ! "—
 Freeze, freeze, O icy wind !
 LUCILLA's cap's awry !

" FAIR."

B LOW, blow, Etesian gale !
      LUCILLA's cap is straight ;
Fill fast the flowing sail
Of happy man and mate.

"What is it, Dear ?—A plate ?
      Do taste this potted quail ?"
Blow, blow, Etesian gale !
LUCILLA's cap is straight.

" More sugar ?—No ?   You're pale.
      My Own, you work too late !
Ah me, if *you* should fail !
      I'll see you to the gate."—
Blow, blow, Etesian gale !
LUCILLA's cap is straight.

TO ONE WHO BIDS ME SING.

" The straw is too old to make pipes of."
—Don Quixote.

YOU ask a " many-winter'd " Bard
 Where hides his old vocation ?
I'll give—the answer is not hard —
 A classic explanation.

" Immortal " though he be, he still,
 Tithonus-like, grows older,
While she, his Muse of Pindus Hill,
 Still bares a youthful shoulder.

Could that too-sprightly Nymph but leave
 Her ageless grace and beauty,
They might, betwixt them both, achieve
 A hymn *de Senectute ;*

But She—She can't grow gray ; and so,
 Her slave, whose hairs are falling,
Must e'en his Doric flute forego,
 And seek some graver calling,—

Not ill-content to stand aside,
 To yield to minstrels fitter
His singing-robes, his singing-pride,
 His fancies sweet—and bitter !

THE SONG OF THE SEA WIND.

HOW it sings, sings, sings,
　　Blowing sharply from the sea-line,
With an edge of salt that stings ;
　How it laughs aloud, and passes,
　As it cuts the close cliff-grasses ;
　　How it sings again, and whistles
　　As it shakes the stout sea-thistles—
　　　How it sings !

How it shrieks, shrieks, shrieks,
　　In the crannies of the headland,
In the gashes of the creeks ;
　How it shrieks once more, and catches
　Up the yellow foam in patches ;
　　How it whirls it out and over
　　To the corn-field and the clover—
　　　How it shrieks !

How it roars, roars, roars,
　　In the iron under-caverns,
In the hollows of the shores ;
　How it roars anew, and thunders,
　As the strong hull splits and sunders :

And the spent ship, tempest driven,
On the reef lies rent and riven—
How it roars !

How it wails, wails, wails,
In the tangle of the wreckage,
In the flapping of the sails ;
How it sobs away, subsiding,
Like a tired child after chiding ;
And across the ground swell rolling,
You can hear the bell-buoy tolling—
How it wails !

LOVE'S QUEST.

(For a Mural Painting.)

WHENAS the watches of the night had
    grown
To that deep loneliness where dreams begin,
I saw how Love, with visage worn and
    thin,—
With wings close-bound, went through a town
    alone.
Death-pale he showed, and inly seemed to
    moan
With sore desire some dolorous place to win ;
Sharp brambles passed had streaked his daz-
    zling skin,—
His bright feet eke were gashed with many a
    stone.

And, as he went, I, sad for piteousness,
    Might see how men from door and gate
      would move
To stay his steps ; or womankind would press,
    With wistful eyes, to balconies above,
And bid him enter in. But Love not less,
    Mournful, kept on his way. Ah, hapless
      Love !

TO A LADY.

(With a Volume of Herbert.)

I.

W HEN I go
   From my place
   At your feet,
      Sweet,
All I know
   Of your face
   I recall,—
      All;
Being by
   (In the net)
   I forget.
      Why?

II.

Being by,
   I but hear
   What you say,—
      Yea,

Naught am I
        But an ear
        To the word
                Heard ;
Then I go
        And the grace
        Of your face
                Know.

FOR A COPY OF "THE STORY OF ROSINA."

WHAT would our modern maids to-day?
    I watch, and can't conjecture :
A dubious tale?—an Ibsen play?—
    A pessimistic lecture?

I know not. But this, Child, I know ;
    You like things sweet and seemly,
Old-fashioned flowers, old shapes in Bow,
    "Auld Robin Gray" (extremely) ;

You—with my "Dorothy" [1]—delight
    In fragrant cedar-presses ;
In window corners warm and bright,
    In lawn, and lilac dresses ;

You still can read, at any rate,
    Charles Lamb and " Evelina " ;
To you, My Dear, I dedicate
    This " Story of Rosina."

[1] See *Collected Poems*, i, 115.

TO LORD De TABLEY.

(In Acknowledgment of a Volume of Poems.)

STILL may the Muses foster thee, O Friend,
   Who, while the vacant quidnuncs stand at
        gaze,
Wond'ring what Prophet next the Fates may
        send,
   Still tread'st the ancient ways;

Still climb'st the clear-cold altitudes of Song,
   Or ling'ring " by the shore of old Romance,"
Heed'st not the vogue, how little or how long,
   Of marvels made in France.

Still to the summits may thy face be set,
   And long may we, that heard thy morning
        rhyme,
Hang on thy noonday music, nor forget
   In the hushed even-time !

TO LADY DOROTHY NEVILL.

(With a Memoir of Horace Walpole.)

HERE is Horace his Life.   I have ventured
    to draw him
As the Berrys, the Conways, the Montagus
    saw him :
Very kind to his friends, to the rest only so-so ;
A Talker, Fine Gentleman, Wit, Virtuoso ;
With—running through all his sham-Gothic
    gimcrackery —
A dash of Sévigné, Saint-Simon and Thackeray.
For errors or ignorance, haste, execution,
From you, his descendant, I ask absolution.

TO EDMUND GOSSE.

(With a First Edition of " Atalanta in Calydon.")

A T your pleasure here I hold
   " Atalanta, snowy-souled : "
Rather smudgy though,—the gold
Not so brilliant as of old ;
First Edition,—this is plain ;
Monogram of J. B. Payne . . .
Dogg'rel this, but it was reckoned
Metre under George the Second.
Then a man was thought a Bard
If by striving *very* hard
He could write—say once a quarter—
Something just as long, or shorter.
Straight they crowned his head with bay,
Nobles took him home to " tay ";
Maids of honour for his muse
Quite forgot their " P's " and " Q's."
See his name on all the posts ;
People rush to buy in hosts
Tonson's last impression with
Author's portrait, done by Smith ;

All his little words are quoted ;
All his little airs are noted ;
And, if he goes trickling on
From his paltry Helicon,
He is made Court-Footman or,
Possibly, Ambassador !

TO THE SAME.

(With Churchill's " Poems," 1763.)

WHEN CHURCHILL wrote, th' Aonian maid
    He served was scarce of speech afraid ;
    She used no phrase to circumvent
    The homely article she meant,
But plainly called a spade a spade.

Nor was the public much dismayed.
He but his age's law obeyed ;—
    They liked to see the bludgeon's dent
        When CHURCHILL wrote.

'Tis not so now. To-day the trade
Demands the finest Sheffield blade ;
    We use a subtler instrument ;
    We cut for depth and not extent . . .
But would 'twere ours—the Mark they made—
        When CHURCHILL wrote !

TO THE SAME.

(With a Memoir of Horace Walpole.)

HAD I but WALPOLE'S wit, I'd write
    A quatrain here to-day
Should turn the wig of PRIOR white,
    And make e'en HORACE gray;

Or had I STANHOPE'S pen (the same
    That once he gave to YOUNG),
I would as neat a couplet frame
    As e'er was said or sung;

But since I've not, I can't, you know;
    The page must go without it;
This is my latest gift; and so . . .
    And so, that's all about it!

TO THE SAME.

(With " At the Sign of the Lyre.")

" BOOK against book." " Agreed," I said:
    But 'twas the truck of Diomed!
And yet, in Fairy-land, I'm told
Dead leaves—as these—will turn to gold.
Take them, Sir Alchemist, and see!
Nothing transmutes like sympathy.

TO THE SAME.

(With Vincent Bourne's " Poetical Works.")

GOSSIP, may we live as now,
 Brothers ever, I and thou;
Us may never Envy's mesh hold,
Anger never cross our threshold;
Let our little Lares be
Friendship and Urbanity.

TO THE SAME.

(With Goldsmith's " Selected Poems.")

GRUB-STREET is Milton-Street to-day;
 And that *antiqua Mater*
Whom GOLDSMITH served has passed away;
 But is our lot the greater?

Ah no! as some lean rascal hides
 His misery from his betters,
We wrap our trash in parchment sides,
 And call our task-work " Letters."

TO THE SAME.

(With a Copy of Walton's " Lives.")

YOU write your Life of DONNE. 'Twill be
    A masterpiece of sympathy !
Exact, I know, in fact and date,
And skilled to lead, to stimulate,
To show, as you would have him seen,
That morbid, mystic, mighty Dean.

But will you catch old IZAAK's phrase
That glows with energy of praise ?
Old IZAAK's ambling unpretence
That flames with untaught eloquence ?
Will you ?   I pause for a reply,
And you must answer, Friend, not I.

TO THE SAME.

(With Eight Volumes of the Author's Works.)

" *Exegi monumentum.*"

EIGHT volumes !—all well-polished prose,
    Or better verse (as some suppose) ;
In style more playful than severe ;

Moral in tone (*pour qui sait lire*);
All written by my single pen,
And praised by some distinguished men,
But else not widely read, I fear :—

Crown me, MELPOMENE, my Dear!

FOR LOCKER'S "LONDON LYRICS,"
1881.

APOLLO made, one April day,
　　A new thing in the rhyming way;
Its turn was neat, its wit was clear,
It wavered 'twixt a smile and tear,
Then MOMUS gave a touch satiric,
And it became a "London Lyric."

TO FREDERICK LOCKER.

(Dedication of " Proverbs in Porcelain.")

IS it to kindest Friend I send
　　This nosegay gathered new ?
Or is it more to Critic sure ?
　　To Singer clear and true ?
I know not which indeed, nor need ;
　　All three I found—in You.

TO EDMUND CLARENCE STEDMAN.

(Dedication of " At the Sign of the Lyre.")

NO need to-day that we commend
        This pinnace to your care, O Friend !
You steered the bark that went before
Between the whirlpool and the shore ;
So,—though we need no pilot now,
We write your name upon the prow.

TO BRANDER MATTHEWS.

(With a Volume of Verses.)

IN vain to-day I scrape and blot :
  The nimble words, the phrases neat,
  Decline to mingle or to meet ;
My skill is all foregone—forgot.

He will not canter, walk or trot,
  My Pegasus.   I spur, I beat,
        In vain to-day !

And yet 'twere sure the saddest lot
  That I should fail to leave complete
  One poor . . . the rhyme suggests " con-
    ceit ! "
Alas !   'Tis all too clear I'm not
        In *vein* to-day.

TO THE LATE H. C. BUNNER.

(With a Volume of Verses.)

WITNESS my hand (and seal thereto)
  All ye who wrong by word or sign,
  This unprotected Muse of mine,
I wish you . . . Something else to do!

May all your bills at once fall due!
  May She, whose grace you seek, decline!
        Witness my hand!

But you, acute, accomplished, true
  And *candid*, who in every line
  Discern a spark (or sparks) divine
Be blessed! There's good in store for you,—
        Witness my hand!

TO GEORGE H. BOUGHTON, R. A.

(With a Volume of Verses.)

S PRING stirs and wakes by holt and hill;
In barren copse and bloomless close
Revives the memory of the rose,
And breaks the yellow daffodil.

Look how the spears of crocus fill
The ancient hollows of the snows,—
Spring stirs and wakes !

Yet what to you are months ?   At will
For you the season comes or goes ;
We watch the flower that fades and blows,
But on your happy canvas still
Spring stirs and wakes !

TO RICHARD WATSON GILDER.

(With a Volume of Verses.)

OLD friends are best !   And so to you
    Again I send, in closer throng,
    No unfamiliar shapes of song,
But those that once you liked and knew.

You surely will not do them wrong,
    For are you not an old friend, too ?—
        Old friends are best.

Old books, old wine, old Nankin blue ;—
    All things, in short, to which belong
    The charm, the grace that Time makes
        strong,—
All these I prize, but (*entre nous*)
        Old friends are best !

TO LAURENCE HUTTON.

(With a Volume of Verses.)

THERE is no " mighty purpose " in this
book.
Of that I warn you at the opening page,
Lest haply, 'twixt the leaves you careless look
And finding nothing to reform the age,
Fall with the rhyme and rhymer in a rage.
Let others prate of problems and of powers;
I bring but fancies born of idle hours,
That striving only after Art and Ease,
Have scarcely more of moral than the flowers
And little else of mission than to please.

EPIGRAMS.

On the Poetry of Artifice.

WITHIN this verse, said Dick, you see
 There's not a single " B " or " D ":
Why not (quoth Ned) go farther yet,
And leave out *all* the alphabet?

On Didactics in Poetry.

Parnassus' peaks still catch the sun ;
 But why—O lyric brother !—
Why build a Pulpit on the one,
 A Platform on the other?

On a Catalogue Raisonné.

I doubt your painful pendants who
Can read a Dictionary through ;
But he must be a dismal dog
Who can't enjoy this Catalogue.

VERSES WRITTEN FOR THE MENU OF THE OMAR KHAYYÁM CLUB.

"It does not appear there was any danger in holding and singing Súfe Pantheism, so long as the Poet made his salaam to Mohammed at the beginning and end of the Song."—FITZGERALD'S *Preface to Rubáiyat*, 1872.

SALAAM to OMAR! we that meet to-night
Have bid Black Care be banished, and
 invite
The Rose, the Cup, the not-too-ancient Jest,
To help and cheer us, but beyond the rest,
Peaceful Digestion with its blissful Calm.
Therefore to OMAR once again—SALAAM!

SALAAM to OMAR! Life in truth is short
And mortal man of many ills the sport;
Yet still th' Oasis of the Board commends
Its vantage-ground for cheerful talk of friends,
And brings Oblivion, like an Eastern Balm.
Therefore to OMAR once again—SALAAM!

HILL AND VALLEY.

HE.

" COME, let us climb to the height,
Peak after peak in the sun,
As the rays brighten, grow rosy and lighten,
Now that the thunder has done.

SHE.

" Nay; through the leafage, the light
Gentlier glimmers below;
See through the valley the rivulets sally,
Singing aloud as they go.

HE.

" Grandly, ah ! grandly the hill
Broke the black storm on its crest ;
All the cliff under went leaping the thunder,
Growling away in the west.

SHE.

" Here it is restful and still ;
Only the drops from the trees,
Where the shades darkle, fall slowly and
sparkle,—
Here there is solace and ease.

He.

"Child, but the eagle above,
  Now that the mists are withdrawn,
Never wing-weary, sails up from his eyrie,
  E'en to the eye of the dawn.

She.

"Ah! but below us the dove,
  Crooning for joy on the nest,
Fills with soft slumbers the leaves without
    number;
  Shadow and quiet are best."

"ROSE, IN THE HEDGEROW GROWN."

" ROSE, in the hedgerow grown,
         Where the scent of the fresh sweet hay
Comes up from the fields new-mown,
You know it—you know it—alone,
    So I gather you here to-day.

" For here—was it not here, say?—
    That she came by the woodland way,
        And my heart with a hope unknown
                    Rose?

" Ah yes!—with her bright hair blown,
    And her eyes like the skies of May,
    And her steps like the rose-leaves strown
        When the winds in the rose-trees play—
    It was here—O my love!—my own
                    ROSE!"

A BALLAD OF ANTIQUARIES.

THE days decay as flower of grass,
 The years as silent waters flow;
All things that are depart, alas!
 As leaves the winnowing breezes strow;
 And still while yet, full-orbed and slow,
New suns the old horizon climb,
 Old Time must reap, as others sow:
We are the gleaners after Time!

We garner all the things that pass,
 We harbour all the winds may blow;
As misers we up-store, amass
 All gifts the hurrying Fates bestow;
 Old chronicles of feast and show,
Old waifs of by-gone rune and rhyme,
 Old jests that made old banquets glow:—
We are the gleaners after Time!

We hoard old lore of lad and lass,
 Old flowers that in old gardens grow,
Old records writ on tomb and brass,
 Old spoils of arrow-head and bow,

Old wrecks of old worlds' overthrow,
Old relics of Earth's primal slime,
    All drift that wanders to and fro :—
We are the gleaners after Time !

ENVOY.

Friends, that we know not and we know!
    We pray you, by this Christmas chime
Help us to save the things that go :
    We are the gleaners after time !

TRANSLATIONS.

REGRETS.

(After Joachim du Bellay.)

ALAS! where now doth scorn of fortune
hide?
And where the heart that still must conqueror
be ;
Where the strong hope of immortality,
And that fine flame to common souls denied?

Where is the joyance which at eventide,
Through the brown night the silver moon could
see,
With all the Nine, whenas, in fancy free,
I led them dance, some sacred stream beside?

Dame Fortune now is mistress of my soul,
And this my heart that I would fain control,
Is grown the thrall of many a fear and sigh.

For after-time no more have I desire ;
No more within I feel that ancient fire,
And the sweet Muses turn from me and fly.

261

REGRETS.

(After Joachim du Bellay.)

HAPPY the man, like wise Ulysses tried,
    Or him of yore that gat the Fleece of
    Gold,
Who comes at last, from travels manifold,
Among his kith and kindred to abide!

When shall I see, from my small hamlet-side,
Once more the blue and curling smoke unrolled?
When the poor boundaries of my house behold—
Poor, but to me as any province wide?

Ah, more than these imperious piles of Rome
Laugh the low portals of my boyhood's home!
More than their marble must its slate-roof be!

More than the Tiber's flood my Loire is still!
More than the Palatine my native hill,
And the soft air of Anjou than the sea!

TO MONSIEUR DE LA MOTHE LE VAYER, UPON THE DEATH OF HIS SON.

(After Molière.)

LET thy tears flow, LE VAYER, let them flow :—
　　None of scant cause thy sorrowing can
　　　accuse,
Since, losing that which thou for aye dost lose,
E'en the most wise might find a ground for woe.

Vainly we strive with precepts to forego
The drops of pity that are Pity's dues ;
And Nature's self, indignant, doth refuse
To count for fortitude that heartless show.

No grief, alas ! can now bring back again
The son too dear, by Death untimely ta'en ;
Yet, not the less, his loss is hard to bear,

Graced as he was by all the world reveres,
Large heart, keen wit, a lofty soul and rare,—
Surely these claim immitigable tears !

THE BALLAD OF BITTER FRUIT.

(After Théodore de Banville.)

IN the wood with its wide arms overspread,
　　Where the wan morn strives with the wan-
　　　　ing night,
The dim shapes strung like a chaplet dread
Shudder, and sway to the left, the right ;
The soft rays touch them with fingers white
As they swing in the leaves of the oak-tree
　　browned,
Fruits that the Turk and the Moor would
　　fright,—
This is King Lewis his orchard ground.

All of these poor folk, stark and sped,
Dreaming (who knows !) of what dead despight,
In the freshening breeze by the morning fed
Twirl and spin to the mad wind's might ;
Over them wavers the warm sun bright ;
Look on them, look on them, skies profound,
Look how they dance in the morning light !—
This is King Lewis his orchard ground.

Dead, these dead, in a language dead,
Cry to their fellows in evil plight,
Day meanwhile thro' the lift o'erhead
Dazzles and flames at the blue vault's height ;
Into the air the dews take flight ;
Ravens and crows with a jubilant sound
Over them, over them, hover and light ;—
This is King Lewis his orchard ground.

Envoy.

Prince, we wot of no sorrier sight
Under the whispering leafage found,
Bodies that hang like a hideous blight ;—
This is King Lewis his orchard ground.

"ALBI, NE DOLEAS."
(Hor. i. 33.)

L OVE mocks us all.   Then cast aside
    These tuneful plaints, my Albius tried,
For heartless Glycera, from thee
    Fled to a younger lover.   See,—
Low-browed Lycoris burns denied.

For Cyrus; he (though goats shall bide
With wolves ere she in him confide)
    Turns, with base suit, to Pholoë:—
        Love mocks us all!

So Venus wills, and joys to guide,
'Neath brazen yolk pairs ill-allied
    In form and mind.   So linked she me
(Whom worthier wooed) to Myrtale,
Fair, but less kind than Hadria's tide,—
        Love mocks us all!

[NOTE :—The two following pieces were Nos. 1 and 3 in a sequence of four *Songs of Angiola,* of which two only are reproduced in the first volume of *Collected Poems* in this issue. As, however, Nos. 1 and 3 have more than once been enquired for, they are here reprinted for the convenience of those who desire to possess the entire series.]

A SONG OF ANGIOLA ON EARTH.

THIS is my Lady's throne :—
 Among green leaves, in bowers
  From sunlight fenced with care
By great boughs overgrown ;
 Her feet are deep in flowers,
  They fall around her hair ;
There is no bird nor sylvan thing
But stays to listen, if she sing
  Before I seek her there.

This is my Lady's face :—
 A cloud of yellow hair
  Stands round about her ear ;
She hath a mouth of grace,
 A forehead white and fair,
  And blue eyes very clear ;
Lids that go over while I see,
And shut the world away from me,
  Because she is so dear.

This is my Lady's dress :—
  In fine silk fairly fit,
    Blue as an egg is she ;
Broad bands her shoulders press
  With dark devices knit,
    And small pearls curiously.
A silver girdle holds her waist,
Whereon these words are rightly traced :—
    A true man taketh me.

This is my Lady's name :—
  It is as soft as air
    And sweet as is the rose ;
No other sounds the same,
  No song is half so fair,
    No music's dying close ;—
But yet, methinks, 'twere sin to say
My Lady's name in open day
    For him to speak who knows.

This is my Lady's praise :—
  Shame before her is shamed,
    Hate cannot hate repeat ;
She is so pure of ways
  There is no sin is named
    But falls before her feet ;
Because she is so frankly free,
So tender and so good to see,
    Because she is so sweet.

This is my love of her :—
　　It waxeth ever new,
　　　Nor waneth any whit ;
This all my heart doth stir,
　　Just that I may be true,
　　　And as she findeth fit ;
There is no thing she bids me do
But I would die to bear it through
　　　Because she asketh it.

Sweet-smelling song of mine,
　　Take cassia, balm, and nard ;
　　　Then hie thee fast with care,
Find out my Lady sweet.
With delicate white feet :—
Before her feet incline,
　　And kiss them—kiss them hard,
Saying " My Master bids thee know,
Madonna, that he greets thee so
　　　Seeing thou art so fair."

A SONG OF ANGIOLA DEAD.

SONG, art thou sad, my Song?
  Thou hast not ease nor sleep,
    Thou art not gay nor glad;
Hast thou not mourned too long?
  Speak to me, Song, nor weep
    Till thou grow gray and mad
For that all Love is fled,
Beauty and bountihead;—
    Song, thou art sad.

Song, ah how fair was she!—
  Days but her praise repeat;—
    Men may seek out with care
Nowhere such eyes to see,
  Nowhere such little feet,—
    Yea, and such yellow hair;
Nowhere like lips, I weet
Kisses thereon to eat;—
    Song, she was fair!

Song, and how sweet she was !
  Spring breezes kissed her face,
    Little leaves kissed her feet,
And the sun kissed, because
  Nowhere in any place
    Thing was to kiss so sweet ;
Nothing so dear as she,
Gentle and maidenly ;—
    Song, she was sweet !

Song, but how good she was !
  There was no word she said,
    But it was wise and good ;
No abject thing but has
  Out from her mercy fed,
    Strong in her pity stood ;
There was no little child
But to her leapt and smiled
    Song, she was good !

How shall we wait, my Song ?
  There is no mirth in cup,
    Nowhere a feast is spread ;
Life is all marred and wrong,
  Grief hath consumed it up,
    Now that our Love is fled :
Earth has no face to see
Pointing my sword for me ;—
    Song, she is dead !

Shall we not leave to sing?
　Nothing can wake her now,
　　Nothing can lift her head;
There is no tune can bring
　Back to her cheek and brow
　　Roses of white and red;
Nothing of ours can stir
Words on the lips of her;—
　Song, she is dead!

Cease then from scent, my Song!
　Change thee thy myrrh for rue,
　　Myrtle for calamus;
Bring for us garments long,
　Weeds to our grief, and strew
　　Dust on the hair of us,
For that all Love is fled,
Beauty and bountihead;—
　Song, she is dead!

NOTES.

NOTES.

A Ballad, Etc.—Page 187.

This poem appeared in the *Saturday Review* for June 19, 1897.

Rank and File.—Page 191.

These stanzas appeared in *The Sphere* for February 3, 1900.

A Postscript to Goldsmith's "Retaliation."—Page 192.

On the 22d June, 1896, these verses were read for the author by the Master of the Temple (Canon Ainger) at the dinner given in celebration of the five hundredth meeting of the Johnson Society of Pembroke College, Oxford. They then concluded with a couplet appropriate to that occasion. In their present place, it has been thought preferable to leave them—like Goldsmith's epitaph on Reynolds—unfinished.

When his pistol miss'd fire.—Page 193.

"He [Johnson] had recourse to the device which Goldsmith imputed to him in the witty words of one of Cibber's comedies: 'There is no arguing with Johnson; for when his pistol misses fire, he knocks you down with the butt-end of it.'" (Hill's *Boswell*, 1887, ii. 100.)

You found he had nought.—Page 193.

" Let me impress upon my readers a just and happy saying of my friend Goldsmith, who knew him [Johnson] well: ' Johnson, to be sure, has a roughness in his manner; but no man alive has a more tender heart. *He has nothing of the bear but his skin.*' " (Hill's *Boswell*, 1887, ii. 66.)

"That he made little fishes."—Page 194.

" If you were to make little fishes talk, they would talk like WHALES." (Goldsmith to Johnson, Hill's *Boswell*, 1887, ii. 231.)

" But read him for Style."—Page 194.

" Thoughts " and " faults," or like rhymes, are to be found in *Edwin and Angelina*, and, for the matter of that, in *Retaliation* itself. But the practice is not confined to Goldsmith; it is also followed by Pope and Prior.

VERSES, ETC.—Page 195.

These were read by the writer at the dinner on Thursday, the 25th March, 1897, Mr. EDMUND GOSSE being then President.

" Our RUSTUM."—Page 195.

Field Marshal Rt. Hon. Viscount WOLSELEY.

" FIRDAUSI."—Page 195.

Mr. EDMUND GOSSE, whose *Firdausi in Exile, and other Poems*, appeared in 1885.

TO ONE WHO BIDS ME SING.—Page 229.

This piece was written in response to a graceful expostulatory villanelle which appeared in *Temple Bar* for February, 1895, and was signed "Cecil Harley."